THE BUDDHA'S TANGO

One Woman...Many Lives
A true story

Dr. Kathy Kangarloo

BALBOA.
PRESS

A DIVISION OF HAY HOUSE

Balboa Press books may be ordered through booksellers or by contacting:

Balboa Press
A Division of Hay House
1663 Liberty Drive
Bloomington, IN 47403
www.balboapress.com
1 (877) 407-4847

Print information available on the last page.

ISBN: 978-1-9822-3014-2 (sc)
ISBN: 978-1-9822-3013-5 (hc)
ISBN: 978-1-9822-3018-0 (e)

Library of Congress Control Number: 2019908316

Balboa Press rev. date: 06/27/2019

I dedicate this book to YOU !
Don't let the music die
Dance, dance, dance passionately to the rhythm of life
Your dance is your message…

Contents

My Page of Gratitude: You Made Me Happen!

First of all, I would like to thank all of the people living in this book, either in body or in spirit. Your presence in my life has made my story unique and powerful. If I have hurt you in any way, I ask your forgiveness; and if you have hurt me through your own confusion, I forgave you long ago.

I thank my grandparents, my mom; my dad; my sister, Kianoush, and her amazing husband Fleming; and my brother, Ali-Reza, and his beautiful wife Shahnaz for playing in the well-written script of my life. You are part of me, and I carry you in my heart forever.

Thank you, my beautiful Negin and my kind Omid, for choosing me as your mother in this exciting reincarnation. I am sure I did something beyond great in my past life to be worthy of your presence in this one.

Tara, Hannah and Persia I love you beyond words and I am sure you know it. I wish to inspire you to live your significance and truth no matter what.

Robin, thank you for being such an amazing son-in-law and for loving Negin so much.

My deepest gratitude to "Frosty," who entered my life in such an irresistible form, teaching me the oneness of all. My tiny but enormous angel in heaven, I bow to you!

Sending my love to Banka and Chuck for challenging me to find my strength and rewrite my existence not once but twice.

My warmest thanks to Zohreh, my special Spirit-Sister; Kelly, my exceptional Spirit- Brother; and Sara, my caring Spirit-Daughter, for being such powerful cheerleaders, believing in my visions and dreams, and helping me to give birth to this baby.

My dear Shirin, thank you for our long, heartfelt conversations about life over hot cups of delicious chai or cappuccino. I love you, my friend.

Dearest Kamelia and Mykal, thank you for sharing your talent with me to create such a beautiful cover for my book.

Dear Kian, thank you for bringing such fun in reading boring legal agreements.

Thank you, thank you, and more thank you to my emerging Om family for your unconditional support and love all these years. You truly make my life worth living and you know who you are.

My extended family and friends all over the world, thank you for making this planet my home and for teaching me the importance of accepting different accents, cultures, and colors.

Thank you, Jean, for sharing your soul with me. You are a big part of this book and my life. Together forever!

Bobby thank you for leading me ever so gently to explore the mystery of Tango.

My heartfelt thanks to the readers for taking me into your world and allowing me to walk a few steps with you on your very special path. And may our journey together continue to serve the light in all.

Om and Namaste.

Come with Me

Life is an adventure; explore it.

I would like to take you through these pages as if you are watching a movie. I want you to step into each page and walk with me among the words, meet the people, and feel the essence of each story, wishing to find the similarities and the lessons to help you in your transformation.

Every time you pick up this book to read a sentence, a paragraph, a page, or a chapter, first close your eyes for a few moments, take deep breaths, and imagine dancing through the pages to the symphony of words, lines, pictures, and punctuation. Be open to feel the feelings of each episode, see the pictures of every event, and hear the voices of people living in this book. Catch yourself between the lines, discover the learnings, and be available for transformation.

In punctuations, find your emotions. See the last word in each chapter not as an ending but as an exciting new beginning. Look at each full stop as a continuation. Every single breath, each pause, and every movement of yours is captured in these pages awaiting your acknowledgement and, ultimately, awakening.

We will be connected through these stories energetically. My words of inspiration will sit on your coffee table, nightstand, or kitchen table, in your office or in your purse, to remind you of how magnificent and precious you really are.

Let the tales I share renew you one word at a time. I imagined this book as a stage for our stories to come together and move in the well-choreographed dance of life. I wish this book to be an experience and not a read only.

2

Shall We Dance?

Life is a blessing: receive it.

Before embarking on the journey of writing this book, I sat in meditation for days and hours at a time, not knowing how the process would begin and where we were heading. I had questions and concerns about the path the book will take. How, why, and what—the three inseparable friends—found a perfect playground in my mind. The more I tried to answer them, the more confusion I had to face.

I am a storyteller. It is time to ask the letters to become words and the words to be kind to each other to create sentences. I invite powerful sentences to follow one another and fill up pages to bring my story to life. In every turn of a page, another new, interesting lesson must be unveiled. It is a process of allowing and not doing.

I need to sit back and allow the letters, words, and sentences to flow through me for a remembrance to come alive. I must be available and willing to witness the birth of my memories into forms. Lifeless information is about to come back to life. As long as I trust the process of manifestation, I will be fine. The journey is intense but exciting!

Today, early morning, I reached out to my clear quartz crystals. Holding the male crystal in my right hand and the female crystal in my left hand, I connected to the sky and the earth. I asked for the merge of Shiva (the universal male energy) and Shakti (the universal female energy) in my thoughts, words, and stories for balance and equilibrium. I wanted my life stories to form a simple, easy, effortless, but powerful expression.

May this book be a mirror for you to see yourself clearly, and may the words become stepping-stones to carry you across the ocean of your experiences and to the land of self-transformation. I hope you accept all that is and take the next step to manifest your visions, dreams, and wishes. May you love and appreciate yourself exactly the way you are now and take loving care to accept the picture you have of yourself in your mind.

Be kind to yourself. Know the value of love and believe passionately and undoubtedly that you are not an accident. You were born carrying a unique message into this world with you. It is carved into every cell of your being. Find it, understand it, believe in it, and share it. This universe honors you exactly the way you are today. We are all waiting to hear your exceptional message.

Believe in your uniqueness and exceptionality. You are an incredible gift to the world.

Welcome to My Home Temple

Life is a present: open it.

It is early morning. The weather is cool; it is still dark outside. I am too excited to sleep and too lazy to get out of bed. For a few moments, I stretch my relaxed body, review my life story, and giggle. My hands come to a prayer pose by themselves and land effortlessly on my forehead, and from the bottom of my heart, I thank God and the angels for the contentment I feel deep in my heart and in my life. I am blessed beyond words.

Take off your shoes, and leave your worries outside. Shoes and worries are not allowed in.

My little home is indeed a humble soul-sanctuary. Statues of Buddhas and monks sit in every corner with their eyes closed, smiling in bliss. They are in total agreement with the flow of life. Candles celebrate life in their elaborate dance of fire. They lose the self to serve the light. Silence is prevalent.

The yin energy of the Divine Mother can be felt everywhere. She is present in handshakes and hugs. She embraces us in moments of joy or grief. She stays with us. My home, this blessed space, welcomes every guest with the love and compassion of the Divine Mother. This is where the being embarks on the flight to freedom. The soul-searching begins here but never ends.

A journey to the land of unexpected, unknown, and unplanned is our everyday story.

I feel safe and protected here in the arms of Quan Yin, the goddess of mercy, love, forgiveness, and compassion. She reassures me that all is good and life is beautiful if only I believe. Her presence can be felt in every corner, in every step, and in all that we say and do here. She is the energy of my home temple.

Fresh flowers dancing in glowing crystal vases remind me of the vibrant colors of our auras. Flowers in their silence tell their bittersweet story of the impermanence of this mysterious life. They don't want me to forget how precious, magical, and miraculous but fragile and short my life is. Green plants rooted in earth, grounded in their stunning pots, gladly show off their beauty and sassiness. They remind me of being content and complete by myself first before inviting anyone else into my world. They are experts in the art of giving and forgiving. They are messengers of love—gurus of contentment.

Soft chants and the sound of *Om,* the sweet whisper of the cosmos, transport me to the realm of acceptance, gratitude, and appreciation for all that I have and all that I am now, just now. I know well that there is no becoming; I am who I am, and it is good to be me. *What if* is not allowed in my mansion of greatness; only *what is* may stay. The *is*-ness, the easiness, the effortless existence of all that is—this is where I learn, I share, and I practice the art of being.

I start my day with Surya Namaskar, a powerful stream of yoga moves to salute the sun and to welcome creative masculine energy into my day. I close the day with Chandra Namaskar, a soft flow of yoga poses to greet the soothing energy of the moon for a relaxing night's sleep. This is a daily deep immersion into the energy of the sun god and the goddess moon. It is essential to surrender to the yang energy of the sun to embrace heat, life, and light in the morning. It is as vital to bow to the yin, cool, soft, and cuddly energy of the moon every evening in full gratitude for peace and harmony.

The elements, the root of my reincarnation in this physical body, remind me of the oneness of all. I bow with reverence to the earth for hosting me in this very short but exciting existence with utmost generosity. Every night before drifting to the realm of dreams, I accept all the good, the great, and the magnificent with gratitude and give back the heartache of the day with more appreciation for all the learnings of that blessed day.

My daily mantra simply is, *Lead me where you need me.*

I trust that the energy knows perfectly where to take me. One day I am here to open a grand, thousand-people yoga conference somewhere in the world; the next day, just to open a door for a less fortunate person. Another day, I show up at the right time and in the most perfect scene to feed the crows or save a dying bee begging for its precious life in a puddle of rainwater. It does not matter where I am or what I do; I am present in that moment. I am available.

"Every moment is sacred, and every breath is holy," says Dr. Brian Weiss, my dear teacher.

I see my whole life as a *mala*, a string of sacred prayer beads, of blessings; each prayer bead tells a fascinating story. Without that bead, the story would not be the same. I praise every event in my story and accept the incomplete, imperfect, unfinished, unpolished mala that I am at this time in my life. I am humble and in total awe. Life is a blessing.

More beads are waiting to be added to the string I call life. More experiences are planned to help the conclusion of this ongoing project that is me. I find order in the midst of chaos; I pause, breathe, and simply surrender. I am available. The last bead to be added to the string is the master bead, which carries the script of this life I am living now. I want the master bead to be interesting, fascinating, attractive, and uplifting. I want to leave a mala behind that conveys messages of hope, courage, enthusiasm, and passion; an undying passion for life; and an unending thirst for being alive.

Behind the creation of each delicately life-crafted bead in the string of my mala hides an insightful and significant story that binds them all together. I wish to leave this world and complete this awesome journey with a smile on my face, saying, *It was worth it. It really was!*

Here are some of those stories for you—simple stories to lead me to the completion of my life in form, believing that there is no end but only a continuation. And here we go!

4

Age Seven

Life is a mountain: climb it.

Mom is so beautiful. Today especially, she looks like a movie star, glamorous and stunning. She is a gorgeous woman—young, tall, and slim. Her nails are always polished in jewel tones matching her lipstick. Her beautiful long reddish hair reminds me of a sheer piece of silk dancing in the wind. Her big brown eyes are windows to the empire of dreams. Today, in her long pastel-pink dress, she looks like a princess in a storybook. She is too perfect to be real.

I get lost looking at the different shades of pink feathers on her dress and the matching hat she is wearing—all shades of love showing off in such glamour. It feels like she is dressed in passion. My sister, my little brother, my grandma, my aunt, and I are watching her every step in awe and admiration.

My dad walks out of their bedroom into the living room, where we are all sitting speechless. He looks perfect in his well-fitted black suit and super-polished black shoes. He walks with his head up. There is a sense of pride in his posture. Today is the day of the king and queen's crowning ceremony—the king of Iran's coronation. My dad is one of the organizers of this epic event. My parents are going to attend this historic function.

"Okay, we are leaving. We will be on TV. Make sure you watch the live broadcast."

"Bye! Be good. Do not bother Grandma."

"Bye! Have a nice time. We promise."

And off they go, leaving the house to make history.

Of course, we cannot kiss them goodbye. We don't want to stain the perfection, the flawlessness, and the precision of this picture.

My little heart is pounding. I'm sitting in front of the television not even blinking because it can happen any minute. I don't want to miss seeing them on our black-and-white TV screen, watching colorful history being conveyed in gray tones. We are super-excited, not taking our eyes off the screen even for a moment.

Majestic golden carriages carrying the guests arrive one by one. It seems as if they are floating in the air. Everything is happening in slow motion. The universe wants this moment to last forever.

Beautiful gowns and jewels dress the day—a proud day for the people of Iran. A royal fairy tale is about to be born, and my family is part of it. I am so excited.

* * *

Yes, my dad's job is very important. He works closely with the king and the administration. It means long days at the office, but he rarely complains of being tired. He is a happy person by nature. He takes life easy.

My dad loves to dance. He is a music lover. The first thing he does in the morning is play music. This is how we know Dad is up. He is fun, generous, and easygoing, and he wants us to be happy.

My mom, on the other hand, doesn't seem to be happy. She has migraine headaches most of the time and wants to sleep in her bedroom with closed thick curtains. The room is dark and smells of medicine. She asks us to be quiet. The house goes to silence often so she can rest.

It is hard to make Mom happy. She does not get excited easily. She complains most of the time.

I know things are happening. I hear loud discussions ending with Mom's crying. She has more headaches, and Dad stays at the office longer. He comes home late—very late.

My tummy hurts. I am nervous. I am not sure what to expect. What is going on? No one wants to talk about it. It is hush-hush.

Dad is taking his stuff. He is gone. My tummy aches even more.

We don't talk about it. We don't have therapists or school counselors to explain to the kid in trauma what is going on. You know it is not good to talk about it. People will laugh at us. My tummy aches a lot.

* * *

I enter a writing competition at school. They are going to send the stories to UNESCO. Children from all over the world are competing. I write my story. The story is about a goose who could talk. I let the goose tell my story. Her tummy hurts just like mine. She cannot talk about her mom and dad. Her dad is gone too.

I win first prize, and my little book is published and kept at the school library. Sometimes I wish for the goose to step out of the book and give me a big hug. The goose shares my pain and my tummy ache. She is my friend.

Sometimes I go to the school library and just hug the book. It is comforting to know that the goose knows my story. I hold the book close to my heart and cry. My tummy really hurts, and the goose knows it.

* * *

I enter a children's national painting competition. The judges are looking at my painting. It is a double-decker bus, red in color. I painted a perfect picture of a bus taking a little girl to find a picture-perfect life.

I am sitting on the top deck looking out the window to find an unbroken, happy family of Mom, Dad, and three kids, but I cannot find it. I am by myself, going on an unknown journey. The bus is empty. It is only me on that monstrous bus leaving the reality of the moment and embarking on the mysterious and at the same time magnificent journey of life. I am alone and anxious but quite excited.

No one talks about my dad not being at home, and I am not allowed to talk about it at school. The girl on the bus knows it. Her tummy hurts too. She is nine years old, just like me.

I win the competition, and my painting becomes a national stamp.

I am happy to be able to tell my story by simply inviting the colors to dance on the canvas. This time, I told my story in complete silence and with no words, but people heard it. I won, but still my tummy aches.

* * *

No one knows my secret. Dad does not live at our home. I do not know why we are not allowed to talk about it. I miss the smell of his aftershave in the morning, He wears Old Spice, and I love it. I miss listening to Nat King Cole or Frank Sinatra while he makes his coffee. I miss him whistling to the music and move like a tango dancer in the middle of our kitchen. I miss him so much, but we pretend that everything is okay.

My mom has more migraine headaches, and I cannot eat. But you know, all is good. Let us pretend that nothing has changed.

Let's not talk about it.

Oh boy, my tummy aches even more.

5

More Heartfelt Childhood Memories

Life is unpredictable; accept it.

Let me tell you one of my profound childhood stories. I was five or six, but the picture is still fresh in my mind after all these years.

I am too excited to sleep tonight. Grandma, Grandpa, and I are sleeping in their bedroom. I am little. It is a beautiful summer day, and the whole family is ready to take a trip to the beaches of the Caspian Sea. Our suitcases are packed, lined up by the entrance, impatient and ready to jump in the car. Everything is planned for an impeccable summer vacation.

We are ready for fun. Sandcastles are waiting to be built and stories to be told. Swimming and playing in the sun has always been my favorite thing to do in the summer. Nothing can ruin our vacation. Everything has been planned with such care by my parents and grandparents. They know it all, don't they?

It is early morning. The sun is still in slumber. Grandpa gets out of the bed to go to the kitchen, and of course, I follow him. I am his official shadow. He cannot get away from me, and I don't think he even wants to. We are always together, inseparable. I adore him, and I am his little princess.

The rest of the family is still asleep. We tiptoe out of the bedroom to the living room. He sits on the sofa and gestures for me to sit next to him. He is holding his head in his hands and complaining of a headache. His face is red and his eyes watery. His hands are shaking.

"My dear, sit here with me. Let me lay down for a few minutes," he says to me tenderly.

"Okay, *Agha Joon*." (This is what I call him. It means "Dear Grandpa" in Farsi.)

"Thank you, my little girl. It will be few minutes only. I will be fine. My head hurts."

I ask, "Do you want me to go call Grandma? She can make you tea, and you will feel better."

"No," he replies. "I will be okay. Just sit here and let me rest."

I am quiet. I can hear my breathing. I think to myself, *Is he okay?*

I sit next to him, holding my doll in my arms, daydreaming about our well-prepared trip. I cannot wait! Only few more hours, and we will be on our way.

Grandpa seems relaxed, peaceful, and in a deep sleep. I am happy. He is not in pain anymore. His face has turned white, and his eyes are peacefully closed. But you know what? We don't want to be late. Time to get up, get ready, and go.

I gently call him. "Agha Joon, Agha Joon, I am hungry. Let's go to the kitchen and make breakfast please."

Every morning, he gives me little pieces of delicious fresh bread with cheese, eggs, and a cup of warm chocolate milk. The smell of our breakfast is delightful. It smells of love and caring. He feeds me with his own hands, and every time I eat a bite or drink a sip of milk, he says, "Bravo! This is my girl!" He makes me feel like a hero. Yes, we love each other beyond words. He is my world.

Why he is not responding? I think to myself

"Agha Joon, Agha Joon," I whisper again

He is not moving. His eyes are closed. I lay down next to him and close my eyes, waiting patiently for him to get up.

The sun is rising. My family is getting up one by one. I hear Mom calling everyone to wake up. "We don't want to be late," she says. "Get up, everyone. Let's get ready and get on the road." She sounds so excited and full of energy.

I run to her. "Mom, Agha Joon is not waking up. I am hungry. I want breakfast."

Mom follows me to the living room and touches his hand. Then she is screaming and calling everyone. What is going on? I cannot understand why she is screaming.

"Shh, Mom," I say. "Be quiet. He has a headache. He is sleeping."

Mom is crying and running in circles uncontrollably. I am panicked. Did I do something wrong? He is not moving.

My entire family is weeping. Neighbors are rushing to our home. I still don't understand what has happened to my agha joon.

My idol is gone in a flash, without saying goodbye to me. His body is on the bed, but he is not there. I cannot find him.

My heart aches. I cannot cry or speak. I hold my doll, gazing at him. *Talk to me,* I plead. *Call my name and tell me what a good girl I am. Let's eat breakfast. I miss you already; I miss you so much. How and why did it happen? Where did you go without me?*

* * *

After being in the room so intimately with the angel of death, my view of passing transformed forever at the raw and tender age of five. I was sitting next to him when his soul flew away. I was a witness to a very tranquil shift. The dark, scary concept of death changed to a peaceful transition. I did not even notice the shift. It was that subtle and smooth.

My grandpa laid down, closed his eyes, took a sigh of relief, and never got up. He had a massive stroke at the age of fifty-two and slipped away in total silence, before anyone could notice or help. He flew away on the wings of the angel of death with no resistance. He accepted the divine invitation of destruction so very effortlessly. He flew away while I was with him but not understanding the magnitude of the moment.

This was my first experience staring Lord Shiva, the God of destruction, in the eyes. It was peaceful, easy, and serene. My dear grandpa's contract was up. He accepted the call, and in a blink of an eye, he was gone. I was sitting next to him watching him. He was motionless, relaxed, and in total peace. It was an easy and effortless transition to the realm of nothingness. And his journey continued.

* * *

For days, I sat quietly on his bed in total disbelief, holding my little doll, which he had gifted me.

Why people are crying? I wondered. *Why is everyone in black? Why is he not here? What is death, and what is dying?* It was a new concept, a new reality, a bitter understanding of loss.

Later in life, I learned that death is the only guarantee we have once we are born. Everything else is conditional but death. I learned that all relationships have a sweet beginning and a bitter ending. We might part ways, or if not, one of us goes to the other person's funeral. There is no escape from this truth.

Later, much later in life, I learned that death is not the end but a continuation in another vibration.

* * *

Days are empty without Agha Joon. I miss his hugs. I miss sitting on his shoulders watching fireworks. I want to put my head on his lap watching cartoons. The colorful almond candies are not sweet anymore. The raisin has lost its sweetness too. Nothing tastes the same without my agha joon.

I don't want candies; I only want his hugs, but he is no more. Candies are here, but Agha Joon left. I don't care for almond candies anymore. He took the sweetness of life with him.

I dream of him often. He tells me stories in my dreams, and I love it. We meet in another dimension. His presence is simple; he is softer. I know he is with me. I cannot see him or touch him, but I can feel him. I know he is next to me always and in all ways.

He left physical existence, but for sure, he did not leave me!

After his passing, Grandma moved in with us to help Mom with raising three kids. My grandmother is the best cook in the whole world.

* * *

Now let's fast-forward. I am ten years old. It is about two years after my parents' divorce. We are having a delicious lunch. Dad is visiting, and when he visits, which is almost every day now, our home is happy. Together we eat, talk, laugh, and listen to the new music tapes he buys often. Being with Dad is fun, but still he does not stay. He leaves at night.

We don't know why he has to leave. Remember, we don't talk about it. We all pretend this is normal. He goes everywhere with us. No one knows the truth, and we are quiet about it.

My dad loves to buy things for us. He is very generous.

"Okay, kids," he says with excitement in his voice, "If you have one wish, if you want one thing right now, what that would be?"

Kianoush, my sister, immediately answers, "A violin! A violin for me."

Ali, my brother, screams, "A tricycle! A tricycle!"

I say, "I want to go to India."

"What? India?" Dad asks. "The country? Why?"

"I don't know why, but I want to go to India. Can I? Please, can I?"

Dad laughs.

Mom has this look on her face as if she saw an alien in the kitchen eating her food. "Did she say India? Seriously?" Turning to me, she says, "Your dad is asking you what do you want to have, and you want to go to India?" Then, to my dad again: "India! She is weird. This is odd." My poor mom cannot stop making comments or asking questions.

"I know that is not possible, Mom," I say finally, "but you know what? I can at least wish for it."

It has been a while that I have been thinking and daydreaming about India, not knowing why. The energy of the Motherland has been calling me. But for now, I take my grandma's prayer *chador* (head cover) or a beautiful bedsheet. I wrap the sheet around myself, carefully put a red dot on my forehead in between my eyebrows, wear Mom's shiny jewelry, look in a mirror, and giggle. What I see in the mirror is an ambitious girl in an exquisite sari dancing passionately to Hindi songs. All I want is to be an Indian and go to India.

Is this an improper wish? I don't think so.

"You mean you don't want anything?" says Dad, pulling me out of my India zone. "India is not an option. Do you want me to buy you something as a gift?"

"Yes, yes," I say. "I want a piano. How about that? I want to take piano lessons. Can I? Please?"

Of course, yes, this can happen, but not India.

We laugh and joke about me and my crazy wish. I better forget about India for now!

We are all super-excited for our gifts to arrive. Dad is leaving; it is time for him to go. Every time he says goodbye, I feel tightness in my tummy. I know in my heart this is not normal. Something is wrong. It feels strange.

"I will see you guys tomorrow," he says as he closes the door behind him.

At least Mom and Dad are not fighting anymore. He eats with us after work and then leaves.

I hear my sister tossing and turning in her bed that night; we share a bedroom. She cannot sleep, she is so excited about her violin. I cannot sleep either. When is my piano arriving? Tomorrow? I don't know. I hope I have it soon. All I know is that Dad keeps his promises, and that is enough to know. I smile, hug my pillow, go under my cozy blanket, and fall asleep.

* * *

The next day, my mind is not focused at school. All I am thinking about is my piano. I am not sure when I am going to have it.

We get out of the school bus and run toward home, hoping to have our wishes fulfilled. Are our gifts here now?

Yes, yes, yes! There is a white violin for my sister, a red tricycle for my brother with a loud horn and bright lights (which he loves, by the way), and a glamorous black upright Yamaha piano for me.

Dad is fun. I love him. I told you: he keeps his promises.

Today, I am the happiest girl! My wish is fulfilled.

* * *

Every time I hear a piano playing on the radio, my eyes well up, although I don't know why. I yearn to connect with music on a deeper level, to open a door to a different possibility. A beautiful delicate hand-carved wooden door waits patiently to open.

Dad finds the best piano teacher in town. His name is Mr. Farid. He is a simple little man who creates magic through his fingers. He is blind and has a daughter who is deaf. He tells me sweet stories about their connection. He says Mina (his daughter) cannot hear him, and he cannot see her. So they communicate through touch. He tells me how beautiful she looks.

One day, I ask him, "Don't you feel sad that Mina is not able to hear your music?"

He says, "No, of course she can." He adds, "Mina puts her hands over mine while I play, and through the vibration, she hears the songs. Mina loves piano and my music!"

Mr. Farid is a guru in my life. He takes me out of my body to figure out the world and its magic through my soul. *No, cannot,* and *not possible* don't get a chance in his vocabulary. He is all about *Yes, it is possible!* and *I can!* He lives way beyond physical existence with least accessibilities.

While playing, I get lost hearing the voice of my piano. I am getting to know it intimately. Moving my little fingers randomly, aimlessly, and effortlessly on the black and white keys is the beginning of a much deeper journey than playing music. I am transported, totally gone to another realm. I am in my own la-la land, my favorite zone, a place of no judgment and no fear. I can feel Grandpa here. Almond candies are sweet again; raisins taste delicious now.

Months pass, and I am in love with the songs my piano sings. Music brings immense contentment into my life. I do not need to talk much. I play in silence to tell my story.

My words change form. I am learning how to express myself in rhythms and beats. I don't want to go anywhere. My piano takes me everywhere. It knows the way, and I trust its wisdom. I feel Grandpa's presence while playing music. I tell him everything in a song, and he listens with care.

I talk to him about Mom and Dad. He knows my secret, but he does not pretend it is okay. He is sad too. Grandpa hears my story through music, and he comforts me with the unusual vibration the notes create around me while playing.

Later in life, I learn about the importance of electromagnetic fields and what we feed our aura. Only then does everything make total sense to me. But at the age of ten, just feeling his presence is enough to lead me where I need to be. I am comforted, reassured, and safe. I feel protected, loved, and cared for in Grandpa's arms through the pulsation in my aura.

This is the starting point of my deep connection to the concept of energy. I feel complete freedom from fear and doubt while in that vibration. I feel unshakable.

* * *

My piano becomes my best friend, my love, my voice, and my confidant. Another beautiful chapter opens up in my life. I play with passion. Time loses meaning once I am with my piano. My fingers learn how to tell my story passionately. In silence, I express my feelings loudly. Every day feels like a celebration—exhilarating and exciting.

I win all kinds of local and national awards. Music is my therapist, my guide, and the friend who knows about my parents' divorce. I feel much better when I play music. I fully trust the confidentiality that lives between my little fingers, my heart, the black and white keys, and the powerful element of sound. In my music lives my truth. I embrace my reality and feel utterly authentic when I play.

Notes carry magic into my life. They graciously allow me to express my emotions in the most profound way. The hidden truth comes to life moving to the melody of my life. It dances gracefully in the spotlight of my music. I feel safe, and Grandpa is back.

But still, my tummy aches from time to time. Now I am old enough to know why.

I miss the smell of Old Spice and the music of Nat King Cole in the morning, and it is okay. Life goes on, and I go with it, letting go of resistance.

6

Age Sixteen

Life is a lesson: learn it.

The love for India is getting more palpable. There is a calling, an urge, an undefined longing.

I have neither been to India nor had a friend or a family member who visited India and brought me back fascinating stories. I am clueless about this vague but passionate desire. The wanting is real, but the reason is unclear.

Often, Dad asks me why. Where is this craving coming from? I simply answer, "I just want to go." There is an immense pull, an unreal thirst to discover India. Where does it come from? I have no logical answer but, "I don't know. I really don't, Dad."

Years later, I learn about the unconscious flow of past-life memories into the stream of our conscious present life, and of course, the phenomena of reincarnation. This precious information answers all my childhood queries, and the secret puzzle is solved. While receiving training from my dearest teacher, Dr. Brian Weiss, in the field of clinical hypnotherapy and past-life regression, I explore many of my past lives as a monk in India and Tibet. This priceless information illuminates and simplifies my longing. I know that I have left a piece of myself in India. I miss Mother India as a child misses her beloved mother.

I visit Tibet for the first time in 2004. I find the monastery that had been my home in one or many of my past lives. This monastery is a hidden treasure in the mountains quite far from Lhasa. It is not a tourist spot but a small, simple home in the mountains, far away from the sophistication of the cities. I know the directions to the place without a map and direct the driver to take us there. The driver is astonished by the precise information I have.

When I enter the courtyard, I exactly know where my room is, and the monastery feels like home. I sit in meditation under a tree for about three hours motionless, watching the movie of one of my past lives. It is comforting and soothing. I am home.

* * *

"Dad, do you think I can ever go to India?" I asked, persistent as always.

"Yes, of course, it is doable. After you finish your college, go for a visit. I will arrange it for you."

"Really, Dad? Promise?"

"Yes," he says. "I will send you after your graduation. I promise." He always keeps his promises.

"Again the India subject?" Mom chimes in. "This is so unusual. Where did we go wrong? No Europe or America ... she wants to go to India! So strange!" There is a deep sense of shock in her voice. She really does not get this, and I don't blame her.

The Iranian belief system does not support the law of reincarnation. When you die, you are no more, and you go either to hell or heaven. End of story. So better be good.

If I had been born into an Indian family, my story would have been completely different, because Hinduism is all about reincarnation and multiple lives on Earth. So my life turns out to be a cosmic joke—born into an Iranian family with Indian beliefs. God had a different plan for me for sure! He made my life spicy and rather interesting.

Hearing my mom's comments is not easy, so I leave the room. I don't want to talk about it. I dream passionately of the day I will fly to India. Another valuable lesson I learn later in life is about the importance of details in our wishes. My dreams and visions about India are detailed and meticulous.

* * *

Summer is approaching. I will be seventeen soon. I have been winning many local and national awards for playing piano, and we have been talking often about me pursuing music in a more professional way. But it will happen if and only if my mom agrees.

"Do you want to go to Europe this summer and see if you can pass the entry test for the school of music in Vienna?" Dad asks.

What? Am I dreaming? "Yes, of course, I would love it!" I respond with so much enthusiasm, I am nearly jumping out of my skin

But Mom does not seem happy with the suggestion. No surprise.

"Why Vienna?" she asks. "She is a good student. She can get into any university in Iran to become a doctor, an engineer, or a lawyer. It is a waste if she goes to music school."

She is talking, and I am quietly listening. *God, please let my dad win this argument, please.*

"She might forget about India if she likes Vienna," Dad replies.

Mom nods in discontent. "Let's hope she does."

* * *

Summer is here, and I am going to Europe. I am preparing to visit London, Rome, and Vienna. Dad won, and I am on my way. How exciting this is!

"I am sure once you see Europe, you will never think of India," Dad says with such assurance.

"We'll see, Dad."

I am thinking to myself and repeating it over and over to make sure I am not dreaming: *Piano for my whole life? Me? A piano player?* The depth of my happiness is unmeasurable. I live and breathe piano.

My luckiest day is here. We are at the airport. I am excited, scared, happy, anxious, and thrilled. I am a cocktail of uncontained emotions.

My dad keeps talking about the importance of the test I have to be prepared for.

"Yes, Dad. I will do my best. I promise." I kiss them all goodbye and promise my dad to call him when I arrive.

* * *

21

What a beautiful place! The weather is neither warm nor cold. It is delicious.

My cousin lives in Vienna with his son and his sweet Austrian wife. They pick me up from the airport, and we go to a charming little restaurant.

I am very excited to explore what is next. I am ready to jump to an unknown future. The world of music is opening its arms to me. I am blessed!

Life is awesome. I love it here. Music runs in the veins of Vienna, feeding the land, flowers, and trees and refreshing my soul. This is home for music lovers like me.

My cousin arranges a meeting with a professor at Vienna's school of music. The next day, I have an appointment for an interview and probably a test, depending on the professor.

I dress nice. My hair dances on my shoulders, reminding me of being free and fluid. I walk with confidence and poise. I pack my music notes and my glasses in a small briefcase, shine my shoes, and prepare to take the next life-changing step. I am eager to meet my future.

* * *

A dignified gentleman greets me in German, and I just bow my head in respect. He points at an ancient but beautiful reddish-brown grand piano in the center of the room and invites me to play a piece for him. I lose myself in the moment. I am not playing; I am telling my life story through the sound of the piano.

I am lost in the music, telling my whole life story to the professor, to the walls, to that thick old red and gold curtain, and to the peacefulness of the room. I want all of them to hear the story of my life. I have Grandpa, the goose, the stamp, my secret poetry book, and my awards in that moment close to me. They all help me to bring my story to life. They sing, and I play the song of my life. I take the professor with me on this journey.

This is not about the notes and the music; this is about me. I want to be heard. *Listen to me, hear me, and accept me with my wounds and wonders. Feel the love and the intimacy between the piano, the music, and my spirit. Dear professor, please allow me to be me!*

His eyes are closed, and he has a tender smile on his lips. His wrinkled face lights up. He is in the moment with me, and I am totally immersed in my element. We connect. We connect deep. Our souls meet somewhere outside that dark room, and he recognizes me through the eyes of music.

He congratulates me, commenting about my style and knowledge. He is pleased, and he welcomes me to join the school.

I successfully pass the practical and theory tests. I am exhilarated. I cannot wait to go back to Iran, pack my bag, come back to Vienna, and start the music school. I do not want to be a doctor, a lawyer, or an engineer, but I surely can play music.

I need a phone. I have to find a phone now. I must call my dad

We go to my cousin's home, and I call my dad, screaming with happiness. My voice is filled with joy, pride, and excitement. I am going to be a musician. No: I am going to be the music!

My dad is beside himself. I have never felt such joy in his voice. He won. Yes, this was the happiest day of his life too.

* * *

In a few days, I am back home, ready to find my life purpose in music. I am so happy and proud of my hard work and dedication to the element of sound. It is not easy to get admission to that music school, but I did it, thanks to my amazing teachers. I had the best teachers along the way. They prepared me for this day. I am filled with gratitude.

I cannot stop talking. I talk nonstop all the way from the airport to our home in the car. My dad is super-happy. Mom is just listening, and I know the last word is always hers. I am doing my best to convince her.

We get home. She is still listening. Finally, this is what she says: "I am so proud of you. You have tried, and I am very happy to know that you have been accepted to attend such a prestigious school. Yes, it is impressive. But!"

But what? I think to myself. I have lost words ... no ... I have lost me. Where did I go? I take a deep breath. What is she going to say? But what? *Please don't say no, please, please say yes, Mom.*

My brain is foggy, not knowing what to think. My heart has lost its rhythm. My breath cannot find its way to my heart. My soul is running aimlessly from our kitchen table to Vienna and back, all in less than a pulse, and my eyes are closed, not allowing me to see the picture Mom is painting.

And she continues: "But since you are an A student, it is better for you and your future to choose a more professional field and practice piano on the side as a hobby. It is a total waste of time for you to become a musician.

Oh my God. My tummy is in knots. It hurts so much! Is she serious? Waste of time to graduate from the best school of music in the world? Is it a waste of time to be an artist? Is it a waste of time to live happy? How about considering being *me* a waste of my time? All I want is to be *me*! Does she get this? I do not think so. She says no to India and now no to piano!

She has the last word. I am not going. She called my love for piano waste of time, and she named my beloved a *hobby*!

Mom adds, "Are you even thinking about your future?"

"Yes, of course, Mom. What do you mean?"

"You are a very good student, Kata. You have all As."

"So?"

"Don't you think you must pursue your studies in a more professional field? Music is just a hobby, not a profession!"

"What? Mom, what are you talking about? Music is my life! It cannot be my hobby."

"Oh yes it can. This school is not a wise idea. You are going to ruin your future, wasting ten or twelve years of your life to learn piano only."

"*Only*? I don't want to be a doctor. I hate being an engineer or a lawyer. I want to be a musician!"

"That is not a job, do you understand?" she says. "You must study."

Here we go again. I cannot go. There is nothing to discuss anymore. I am going to stay and go to school in Iran.

"My dear, if your mom does not agree, you better stay and maybe after college graduation follow music in a more professional way," Dad says in disappointment. He lost. We both lost.

* * *

My world is shattered again. The dream is ending, and I am back to the world of what is right and what is wrong. Dos and don'ts are creeping in again. This is not my ideal world. Why can't I follow my heart?

I am here to create my own world. I know that I am not an accident. I have a purpose—a unique one. The road is winding, and the path is not paved, but I know in my heart that the world needs me. I want to be pleased and gratified with my life in order to contribute to the joy in the world. I respect all doctors, engineers, and lawyers who have found their purpose in their profession, but an unhappy doctor, miserable lawyer, or depressed engineer is not who I want to be. I want to be a happy, cheerful, content woman, and I can find all of these in playing piano.

Is this a lot to ask? I just want to be me! Allow me.

7

Govinda Restaurant

Life is a treasure map. follow it.

It is the last year of high school. I study hard. I am getting ready to take the university entry exam.

"Eat!" Mom demands over and over again

The sight of kabob is sickening. I cannot eat meat for breakfast, lunch, and dinner. Yet doctors forbid me from eating greens and fruits. They believe vegetables are poison for a person with a stomach ulcer, so they prescribe chicken or beef three times a day. It really disgusts me.

"I can't, Mom. I really cannot stomach meat anymore."

"Try one bite," she insists.

"No, I can't." I throw up everything I eat. My stomach hurts so much. My only comfort is playing piano for hours after returning from school. I play piano and write poems in my own silence, and I do not share my writings with anyone. When I write or play piano, I find my sacred space. I am happy, and my stomach feels calm and relaxed. It is my sanctuary, my escape, my refuge. When I am with my "hobby," I feel safe and protected.

How can Mom call this amazing gift a hobby? I still do not understand.

"I found the best doctor," Mom says with a smile on her face. She lights up talking about this new doctor, and the glow on her face is trying to tell me something. But I am tired of going to doctors. So many different medications and the kabobs I eat. I pray for a divine interference. I need help from somewhere else. Something has to change drastically.

"Nothing works, Mom. My body is tired. I hate the food I eat. I cannot do this anymore. We are going in circles. Something has to change, but I do not know what. I need a miracle."

"This doctor is the answer to your prayers. I heard many great things about him. Let us try," she insists.

"I don't want to go to another doctor appointment. I am done, Mom! Please, let me be."

"This is the last time, I promise you," she said. "This one works. I know it."

For sure, she knows something I do not. She is certain about something that I am not.

We get ready. I am in such excruciating pain. We get in the car not knowing that this appointment will change my life forever.

Everything is in divine order, and all happens according to divine timing. A miracle is about to be born.

We are sitting in the waiting room listening to the *tick-tack* of an old clock on the wall. The energy of the room is heavy; the air feels dense. Time has slowed down since we walked in. The universe is going to have a heart attack any moment. It feels as if the earth is breathing heavily. The breath is labored, and the sound of the old clock is warning us of the thick, heavy energy dumped in the room.

This place is dressed in pain and sadness. Every piece of furniture is crying in agony. The room has no windows with a few unmatched, random pictures on white walls. A few dusty plastic plants are neglected here and there. The space is sinking in a cold, gray, gloomy aura, and of course the doctor is never on time. Another man is sitting across from us, waiting to see the doctor. He is watching me in silence. He is quiet but observing. I can feel the depth of his look on my body. He is here for a reason. He has a mission. I call him the man –angel!

It feels as if I am sitting on a bed of nails. Pain is my companion wherever I go. I cannot sit still. I have an unbearable pain in my tummy. It hurts; it burns. My body is not happy. I cannot breathe. I cannot suppress my tears any longer. I burst into tears and cry quietly. I am desperate, tired, hungry, starving, and cannot eat that kabob anymore.

God, angels, somebody, anybody, help!

* * *

"What is going on with your daughter?" the man-angel asks.

"Incurable stomach ulcer; an undying pain," Mom says softly.

"This is an easy fix. You don't have to suffer so much, dear," he replies. Then, turning to Mom, he asks, "What do you feed her?"

"Different kinds of kabob. Chicken or beef, of course," Mom answers with confidence.

"No, she must become a vegetarian and start meditation," the man-angel insists.

What? What did he say? What did I hear? Vegetarian? How? A meal without that nasty meat? Meditation? What is meditation? My mind is racing.

I love this man already. *Who is he? Where did he come from? I bet he knows the goose, or maybe he is someone hidden in my painting.* Now I am all ears listening to him.

"You must cleanse and calm your body and mind. You need to be quiet to reflect," he adds.

Oh God, a miracle is about to happen here. My prayers are heard and answered. He is my man-angel!

He asks for a piece of paper and writes something on it. This piece of paper is my ticket to freedom. This little piece of paper was sent from heaven. I don't even read the paper. I fold it and put it in my pocket like a treasure map.

"Go to the address on the paper," he tells me. "Eat all vegetarian food, learn how to prepare vegetarian meals, and study meditation there. You will end this misery in no time." He adds, "This pain is your teacher. Listen to it. Put your hand in the hand of your angel. Trust your heart and keep an eye on the signs you receive along the path. Do not doubt. Keep on walking. You will be there. The road will take you where you need to go. But you must follow the path."

The obstacle becomes your path only if you follow the signs.

"Path? Which path?" I ask, weeping in hopelessness.

"You will know," he responds. "Just follow the signs and listen to your guides."

Something in his words makes me trust him. He is wrapped in such bright light. I am lost in the glow he embodies. His smile is angelic. I am sure the goose in the book or the girl on the bus living on the stamp sent him to help me. He is the sweet answer to my daily prayers.

For the first time in a long time, I am filled with hope. Finally, I can see a candle lit in the darkest room ever. Yes, mom was right—the best doctor visit ever!

Of course, my brain disrupts the ecstasy I am experiencing. This is the discussion between my anxious brain and my happy heart:

> Brain: *Why are you listening to this stranger? Who is he? What does he know? He doesn't have an ulcer. He is not a doctor. Just another patient sitting in the room.*
>
> Heart: *Oh, maybe his daughter has. Who knows? What do you know, brain? I am going to listen to him and follow the unknown mystery path anyway!*
>
> Brain: *You are an idiot. Go to the doctor and fill the prescription. Why do you listen to this man?*

And the conversation goes on and on. But I have no choice. I have to pause, listen to my heart, surrender, and follow the signs.

I am not going to doubt him. I will try anything. At this point, I have nothing to lose but discomfort, disease, and despair, my heart gently whispers, trying to convince my mind. And the conversation between the two goes on and on. Sounds familiar, doesn't it?

* * *

Mom is totally against the idea. But I am not. For once, I take control of my life. I am going to do it. It feels right. I can feel my tummy smiling. *Finally, girl, you are being guided on the right path.* This is how the stumbling block changes the path.

"Vegetables are not good for you," Mom insists.

"Meat is not either, Mom."

From that day on, I refuse to eat meat. I become a vegetarian, which scares the heck out of my mom, grandma, and dad. They all think I am going to die, and soon.

They all try in their own special way to convince me that the man is wrong, but something in my heart pushes me to go forward.

From a very young age, I've listened to my heart. That is how I wrote, painted, and learned piano. I did all that because of the green flashing light in my heart that read *Go!* My heart has always been my guru, my teacher, and my wise master. This does not mean I never make mistakes. Don't get me wrong: I've made hundreds of big and small mistakes in my life. But all of them turned out to be valuable lessons.

I choose free fall over hanging in fear from the side of a cliff. Taking chances with people, situations, and events has been my strength along the path. I allow myself to fall, believing that every time I get up, I am an inch taller, a bit wiser, and less afraid. There is a deep sense of "I am protected" in me that I cannot deny. I am forever grateful to the energy that has guided me through the dark passages of my life and back to the light.

The day at the doctor's office was one of those days. I knew in my heart this man was God-sent. He was there to put me on my path even though I did not know what the path was. He pointed the way, and I followed the signs with ultimate trust.

We all have these moments of enlightenment, but most of us do not believe in abstract and metaphysical signs. We generally look for tangible, solid evidence. But in most cases, there is no concrete evidence. We must take a chance, trust our intuition, and decide to turn right or left. The most important thing is to be open and ready to bear the consequences and to take responsibility for all possibilities.

For example, in my case, if the doctor is wrong, he is not to blame. I must take the responsibility to admit "I did it my way," which gives me the strength and confidence to go forward. Playing the role of victim and blaming others takes the authority, the Shakti (the power), off and adds unbearable weight to our shoulders. Doubt is a heavyweight champion, and it wins most of the time. In the end, it is our decision that counts, and it is our growth that is in need of never-ending undertakings.

Life is not a project; it is an experience. We do not come to this world with a user's manual. Fortunately, we are given free will to choose. The law of karma brings us together or puts us on a special, unique path, but it is up to us to say yes or no to the offerings of karma. If we say yes, life changes and creates another set of responsibilities; if we say no, we manifest a completely different reality.

So yes, there is the law of karma combined with our free will which designs the master plan of our lives. We ultimately live it our own way.

* * *

I am totally devastated and confused but decide to go with my heart and not with the doctor's brain, my mom's, or even my own. It sure is time to say yes to my gut feeling, follow the signs, and be ready for what awaits me on the unknown, never-walked-before path. Oh boy, I am so very ready for it. The time is right. I can feel it in every cell of my body.

Do it—it is your time is written all over me, and I am filled with confidence and power to manifest a pain-free life at last.

The nice man-angel gave me an address to a vegetarian restaurant which is far from my home, but I do not mind the distance. I would go to the end of the world to get relief from this monster pain. *I am going there to learn few vegetarian recipes*, I thought. Life can be very interesting only when we pay attention. I have no idea what I am getting into, and this is the power behind the man-angel's message. Run, possibly fall, but trust that you will be guided.

By the way, the internet or Google does not exist at this time. And Yelp has not born either. Our Google and Yelp are our next-door neighbors, our aunts and uncles, and strangers we meet at shops or parties. Most of them have humongous opinions and no knowledge at all. So I decide to keep this finding a secret and explore it on my own.

I find the restaurant. I walk in, not knowing what to expect. All I care about is: I am here, and I am ready.

The place is decorated in beautiful bright colors, mostly red and gold mixed with vibrant shades of orange and yellow. The smell and the vibration of this place is different from anywhere I have ever been before.

Besides the delightful fragrance of Indian food and all of the naughty, playful spices dancing in the air, there is another pleasant scent that I cannot identify. The aroma makes me feel comfortable. The smell is different but familiar. I feel at home. I've never experienced this fragrance, but I know it. I am not sure from where.

This is a strange but interesting place—a unique Indian restaurant. We eat only after we sing and dance to the rhythm of the drums and bells.

Here lives a sense of calmness and composure. I feel whole and one with the world and everyone in it.

A strong sense of peacefulness lives here. The energy of the room is light and cheerful. Something tells me that I will be fine. No—it whispers into my ear that *I am* fine.

I love the music they play. It makes me happy and relaxed at the same time. We repeat a line over and over, but I don't know the meaning of it. It is all in Sanskrit. I just copy everyone else in the room. They all look so content and comfortable.

Hey, I could not go to India, so India came to me! I am happy—very *very* happy. The man-angel has sent me home! The Goddess is too busy to come to earth herself, so she sends her messengers.

This is a sweet home with a little garden converted to a restaurant. People are happy here. They are welcoming, as if they have known you for years. They are different, simple, and happy.

I see a boy who does not talk. His eyes are usually closed. He sits on a cushion on the floor in a cross-legged pose and plays a little bell softly. When he walks, I do not think his feet touch the earth. He is calm and extremely peaceful. I call him Mr. Love.

I watch him closely, as if I am watching a slow-motion movie or a ballet. He moves gracefully but never talks or makes eye contact. He lives in his own world, content and quiet, wearing a sweet smile at all times. There is a sense of richness and ease in his existence. He does not need much. He reminds me of my favorite line from the Tao Te Ching: "Once a wise man said nothing."

I come here often. Before the meal, a few guys play drums, chimes, and bells. We recite chants and dance to the tunes. I love the rhythm. I enjoy the flow. We move freely and aimlessly.

When I sing and dance here, I feel immersed in an ocean of love. There is a sense of "It's all going to be great!" in the air. No one talks about it, but we all feel it. A sense of contentment that I have never felt before washes over me, allowing me to say to myself, *I am who I am supposed to be. I am in the right place at the right time doing the right thing.* So confusion leaves, and acceptance takes its place.

Feeling immensely blessed to be here, wrapped in a blanket of simplicity and pure love, we sit in stillness after our group dance, enjoying the flow of energy. I am sure the healing happens in this very instant when we all surrender to the perfection of the moment. Only when the mind rests in stillness, enjoying the tranquil silence, can the whisper of the goddess of love be heard clearly. Yes, we can hear her while in silence. We know that she is with us. In fact, she has never been away.

After a few minutes of deep silence, we bring our palms together, say a gratitude prayer, and begin eating quietly. I love to eat in silence. There is an ultimate pleasure when you connect with your food in quietness and appreciation. You create a sense of gratitude while eating in silence which feeds your spirit. Eating silently is not only great for the body, it calms your mind and at the same time nourishes your spirit.

* * *

"Good afternoon, Bhagat."

"Hey, Kathy."

"How are you?" I ask.

"I am fine. How are you doing?"

"Great! I have no stomach ache. All gone! No meat for almost three months, and my body is so happy. Indeed, it is a miracle."

Bhagat plays the drum so passionately, and he is always kind and very helpful to guide everyone. I think he is the owner of the restaurant. I am not sure.

"I am healed, Bhagat. I am so grateful."

"I am very happy for you, Kathy. You are on the path."

What path? What does it mean?

He asks, "Do you want to move in here with us?"

Move where? Into the restaurant?

"Do you live here yourself?" I ask.

"This is not just a restaurant, Kathy," he replies.

"Then what is it?"

"This is a temple. Have you been upstairs yet?"

"No. Take me, please," I say.

"Okay, come with me. Let me show you," he says. "Follow me."

I walk behind him, climbing the stairs, quite excited and utterly clueless, not knowing what is awaiting me.

"Come in," he says. He opens the door.

We are in a magical room with beautiful sculptures. There is a stunning statue of a man playing the flute next to a beautiful woman wrapped in a gorgeous silk sari all adorned in jewels and immersed in merry gold flowers.

"Who are these people, Bhagat?"

"This is Lord Krishna," he replies, bowing his head in Namaste pose. "The god of love with his consort Radha. This is a Hari Krishna temple."

"What temple?" I ask.

"Hari Krishna. We pray to the lord of love."

Oh. Now I can understand the chant: *Hari Krishna Hari Krishna, Krishna Krishna Hari Hari, Hari ram Hari Ram Ram Ram Hari Hari.* So all this time, I have been praying to Lord Krishna unknowingly to take away my pain, and he did it easily and effortlessly, with so much love and compassion.

My hands follow my heart, ending in Namaste pose as well. My head is bowed in thankfulness. My being is treasuring an ultimate trance.

Wow. India came to me! India is here. I am in India! How lucky I am. I am the happiest girl, touched and healed by the lord of love.

I called India from the bottom of my heart, and Mother India responded. She heard me.

Life unfolds in divine order and according to the mystery of divine timing.

I go home in awe and amazement. I cannot wait to share this experience with my mom and, later in the evening, with my dad.

What just happened? I am not sure. All I know is I am healed!

* * *

"Okay, so they are Indians?" Mom asks.

"Yes, a few of them."

"Do they practice Hinduism?"

"Yes."

"They invited you to live with them?"

"Yes."

"What do you want to do?"

"I already told Bhagat that I cannot live there, but I am willing to take care of their garden, since I am going to be a student of agricultural engineering." So from now on, I will not pay for my food. I exchange food with service. I am a proud gardener of Hari Krishna Center in Tehran, and I am loving it.

I am getting prepared and much closer to India, following the treasure map of my life, one step and one turn at a time.

* * *

It has been forty-two years since I conquered the devastating ulcer by practicing yoga, meditation, reiki, and of course, a healthy vegetarian diet. It is gone, all gone! Thank you, man-angel!

The ulcer taught me how precious my body is. It led me to become a total vegetarian and to treat my body with ultimate care, love, and respect. It put me on the path to self-love, self-realization, and self-transformation. Through the changes in my diet, I found deeper respect for all life on earth. I learned that animals are not for eating.

Through challenges created and orchestrated by an unhealthy, always-in-pain body, I realized the importance of health and well-being. The unbearable pain became my vehicle to take me through the dark places and back to the light. The road was steep, narrow, and winding. Sometimes I felt as if there was no end to it, but of course, I was wrong again.

A master bead is being polished. One gentle stroke at a time …

8

Shiraz University

Life is music: find your rhythm and dance to it.

My entire family is beyond thrilled. My home is filled with flowers, cookies, candies, happiness, and joy. This is a big deal. Around 50,000 people take the entrance exam every year, and only 5,000 students get accepted to universities from all over Iran. I am #653 of the first 5,000. Pretty good! With this score, I have the opportunity to enter any university I want. I already chose Pahlavi Shiraz University.

This highly prestigious school is the only international university in Iran located in the city of romance: Shiraz. It is the city of love, poetry, and rose gardens. Shiraz is a very relaxed city; it rests calmly in the arms of intoxicating jasmine flowers. This place welcomes historians, tourists, and lovers from all over the world. The history behind Takht-e-Jamshid, the unmatched nature and the energy of the master-poet, Hafiz, gives an unparalleled charisma to this city. The land is of a very high vibration. "Love is in the air" makes total sense here.

I picked agricultural engineering and food science to connect with nature as my major. You want me to have an engineering degree, Mom? Let it be agriculture. At least I will be working with Mother Earth.

Mom is happy. My plan remains the same: graduate, give her my degree, and fly to India.

I know being an engineer is not in my future. I can totally feel it. I am no engineer by nature. My left brain, the digital brain in charge of calculation and logical thinking, is on vacation in this life. Most of the time, I am under the supervision of my right brain—the part of the brain in control of the three-dimensional senses, creativity, and the artistic aspect of life. But hey, Mom is the boss! End of discussion.

I move to beautiful Shiraz. I live in the dorm, connected with a few girls and having a great time bonding together. This is the beginning of a five-year course, so I better love it!

The school professors are mainly from the United States and the United Kingdom. Classes are taught in English. It is challenging but rewarding to push your boundaries and leave your comfort zone. A deep sense of achievement is thrilling. My classes are mostly outdoors in nature, helping me to cope with the situation.

* * *

While exploring on campus, I discover a room with pale green walls and a big framed picture of Beethoven. Is this a music room? I walk in and see a grand black piano sitting in the center of the room. The piano is the heart and life of these four walls. Here, music is being made and souls are being reunited. I found the magic room!

I immediately sign up to take piano lessons. The professor is incredible; I adore him. Taking piano lessons daily nurtures my spirit. It is the boat that keeps me floating and the air that transports me to the world of imagination and fairy tales. This is the time and the place to be me—an hour of liberation, free from dos and don'ts. I escape for a moment to the world of daydreaming and authenticity. It is my one hour of truthfulness, the time I am allowed to face myself, knowing that the self is still alive somewhere within me. Somewhere deep down is this childlike being, daydreaming of ultimate freedom from forced laws.

I continue self-searching to find the key and unlock happiness. I feel no restrictions here. The energy kind of feels like Govinda, the Indian restaurant in Tehran. This is my new sanctuary. In this space, I am allowed to be me. My fingers awaken the keys, and they sing of freedom and liberation. This is my time to modify the reality that I have been forced to be in—the world that has been planned for me, that I have been ordered to live in. My spirit moves to the dance of ecstasy here while the piano tells us her story.

We are all happy—me, the green room, the piano, and Dr. Amir, my exceptional piano master. He is kind, thoughtful, accepting, and comforting. He can feel my vibration. He is blind, but he sees the world with much clarity. He can see through me as if I am invisible. He knows me, and most significantly, he gets me. The time spent with him is total pleasure. It is uplifting and inspiring. He brings confidence and courage into my world. He opens the door to my heart, reassuring me that I am enough.

* * *

When I arrive to the class, Dr. Amir always recognizes me by my footsteps.

"Katayoun, come in."

I say hello to him and tell him about my day briefly. He asks me to leave the outside world behind and allow the sound of my breath to take me inward. This is where he wants me to be when I play.

He leads me to play from a platform of non-form and no-shape. He directs me to the space within that has never been born and will never die. He wants me to play from the point of power, to connect with the notes fearlessly and play the song of vulnerability entering the zone of courage. He encourages me to live fully.

In his world, all is impeccable. He lives in the company of perfection while in the core of imperfection. Yes, he lives it.

"Okay, Katayoun, take a few deep breaths," he begins. "Find yourself. Do not think; just allow your fingers to touch the keys and gently wake them up. When you are rooted in your element, your fingers will find the right key, and the piano will sing your vibration. The music you hear is your vibration in the form of sound. It is you, only you, present in the pause. This is the realm of perfection; this is where everything is the way it is supposed to be, not the way we want it to be."

Dr. Amir continues, "If and when you enter that space, all doubts, worries, and fears fade away. What you see is extreme passion for life and living. I want you to paint this picture with your fingers, using the black and white keys. Rooted, grounded, centered. The piano is here not to confirm you but to accept you. Do you understand?"

"Yes, I do." I begin playing the story of my soul, his soul, and the soul of the universe combined with the spirit of the green room, all in one song.

Every day at the end of the class, we play together, four hands on the keys. We get lost in the world of time and matter free from consciousness, visiting the reality of *easy*-ness and *is*-ness. We lose ourselves in the music and the vibration it creates. We stay in the now, with no care for the past and no hope for the future. All that matters is the now, this moment, and this instant. The rest does not matter.

I love to be with him. He allows me to be me. There is no pretense but full presence. Our auras melt into each other and into the music. The sound of the piano is the song of independence for both of us. I help him to see what is happening outside. The light is awe-inspiring. In turn, he takes me to the inner world of darkness and quietness. This is where Yin meets Yang.

I run with him through the valleys of light while he walks me through the unknown, mysterious fields of darkness. I, my mentor, and the music become one inseparable being. This is where mind and matter embrace divinity.

The hour goes by so fast. The next student comes in.

"See you tomorrow!" And here goes my life day by day in search of the key to unlock happiness. I'm still in love with India.

9

First Love

Life is beautiful: celebrate it!

It is a gorgeous autumn day. The school year has just started. My roommate and I are exploring every corner of the university grounds. Our campus has a beautiful garden with pink and white roses. We are waiting for the next class to resume, enjoying the season of transformation, the beautiful golden fall.

"He is so cute. Who is he?" My roommate is talking about a handsome guy standing on the other side of the courtyard, talking to a group of new students.

"I don't know him," I answer. "Maybe he's a new student like us."

He is walking toward us now, dressed tastefully in light blue shirt and navy blue pants. He carries a comforting sense of familiarity in his approach. A nice friendly smile complements his shiny brown eyes and light golden-brown hair.

My friend is getting super-excited. "Oh my God, he is coming to us!"

"Hi, my name is Raz," he says.

"Hi, Raz. I am Kathy, and this is my friend Sel," I reply.

He nods and says politely, "My roommates and I are having a simple party tonight at our apartment to get to know a few other new students. Would you like to join us?"

My friend Sel jumps in and replies for both of us: "Sure! What is the address and when? We would love it. Thank you for inviting us."

His mannerisms make me trust him easily.

Sel goes on and on, as if she is delivering a speech. I stay quiet, praying for her to shut up. Eventually, she calms down. We get the address, exchange a few words, and go to our classes. We don't know anyone here, and this may be our first step to meeting interesting people.

After school, we go to our dorm, get ready, and here we go! Our first college party. This is a great chance to meet people, make new friends, and form a new group.

Raz and his two roommates have a cute little home. Three friends share a three-bedroom cozy apartment, a simple student home.

Raz is respectful, handsome, attractive, and very attentive. He chooses the seat next to me and pays close attention to what I say and do. His presence is comforting. I feel no resistance toward him. I would love to spend time together and get to know him.

Our conversation is very interesting. We both passionately talk about music and the effect of it in our lives. He plays guitar and sings love songs; he is a gentle spirit with a velvety voice. He seems to be very romantic and in touch with his feelings and emotions. I like his energy. We are having a great time. A simple, effortless connection is being born.

The evening ends, and he asks if we can meet more often.

"I would love to," I answer.

This evening is the start of a true soul connection that unlocks many doors to immense happiness. It is a reunion of two souls searching for love, passion, compassion, and oneness. What a fabulous adventure! Our story begins right there and then, with no pretense or superficiality. Easily and effortlessly, we swim with the flow.

We spend every evening together. He studies mechanical engineering. We do not share classes. We play tennis in the afternoons, watch basketball and soccer games with our friends, or sit in the library studying. All we want is to be together, and it really doesn't matter when or where. As long as we are together, we are in bliss.

Weekends are great for watching movies and cooking meals. We build our simple love nest based on truth, love, and respect. We decorate it tastefully with music. It is a cozy, warm, and safe togetherness.

I am in love. He is in love. We are totally absorbed in love. It seems as if the whole world is in love. My life is fuller and has a deeper meaning with Raz in it. Being together so effortlessly is the prescription for all diseases and discomforts.

School feels great now, and the city of Shiraz is adding another love story to her credit. Life is magnificent when you allow love into your heart.

No words can describe my feelings. All I can say is, I am living awesomeness! You know what I mean. You have been in love. You have felt it before, haven't you? I am hoping you are in love right this moment. Close your eyes; take a deep breath to feel the feelings and hear the voice of your beloved. It is refreshing. Isn't it?

Revolution

Life is a challenge; face it.

Things are changing rapidly. Aggression, violence, and fear are ruling. Love, poetry, music, and romance have left our country. The vibe of the people has changed. The royal aura of our land has died. What is going on?

Streets are crowded. Sirens go off randomly. Fear is presiding undoubtedly. Something is not right.

People are demonstrating here and there. They are in the streets. We hear anti-regime slogans. Anger and frustration rule every town. People are not happy. They want more.

Schools are closed. Soldiers and revolutionary guards are shooting people. People are dying. What happened to the land of Rumi and Hafiz, of poetry and wine?

I am back in Tehran with my family, and Raz is with his. We cannot see each other often. Being on the street is dangerous. It feels like a nightmare with no end.

People are stressed out and scared. We don't feel safe anymore. Many have guns, and the roar of bullets is devastating.

The king and the royal family have left Iran. Chaos and uncertainty are bitter facts of every day. We live moment to moment.

We don't know what is happening. Nobody knows. We are praying for a miracle, but the reality of the moment is far away from it. When is this nightmare ending? The darkness is creeping in breath by breath. Day by day, we are going further away from peace.

Revolution happens. Many die; many are in prison. The shadow of fear is paralyzing.

* * *

Schools open again, but nothing is the same. Everything has changed. We have guards with guns at our school. One of my classmates, Ali, is now standing at the gate with a gun pointed at us.

"Hello, Ali," I say.

"I am not Ali anymore. I am Brother Ali," he answers without a smile. Is he angry with me? Why? I don't know.

We have been friends for a year. We had classes together. We met at the cafeteria, eating, talking, and laughing daily. What has happened to him? Where did he go, and who is this monster? He changed!

Everything changed with Ali. Our life changed altogether, and for me, Ali is the face of that change, so drastic and with no foundation. It is a superficial change with no understanding of the magnitude of the disaster.

Today, we, the young blood running through the veins of our beautiful country, the students from all over Iran, are filling up the streets to protest. We want our freedom back. Peace is lost. No—it has been stolen from us. We want it back, and we will fight for it.

The monster of fear is ruling, and we are going to end this nonsense. We are young, energetic, and wise. We have the confidence that we can turn the clock back and bring peace and calm to the streets, to the schools, and to our lives. As our grand master/teacher, spiritual leader, and ethical philosopher Zoroaster sweetly said, "I am here to fight the darkness, but to fight the darkness I do not need a sword, I just turn on the light." We use words in the form of peaceful mantras, but they shoot at us. How unfair!

College students are showing up in the streets with slogans of freedom. Soldiers and guards are fighting us with tear gas and bullets. The guards of evil arrest about three hundred of us, and we are in Shiraz jail. It is horrifying. Many girls, in total panic, started their period once we arrive at the prison. The heartless, merciless guards refuse to give them sanitary pads. They are embarrassed and scared. Humanity is wounded and bleeding to death.

Do I want to stay in this country even if I am released from the prison? I don't think so. This is not my home anymore. Who are these mean creatures?

* * *

They kill a few students. The organizers of the protest are dead. Criminal, they are! They answer slogans with bullets. The spirit of evil is growing rapidly.

The government wants us, women, to wear hijab (head cover). We don't want the mandatory hijab. I totally respect women in hijab if it is their choice, but definitely it is not mine. I want my life to be celebrated and not suffocated by unrealistic demands of the government. Wearing hijab or not is very personal, and I want to be able to decide on my way of living. Again, if hijab is your choice for any reason, I respect you totally. Live and let live has been my philosophy forever.

At the scene of the protest, two men grabbed me, pulling my ponytail and throwing me toward each other while screaming into my face, "Cover it! Damn it, cover it!" They were passing me to each other like a ball. I was scared and full of rage toward them and their ignorance. I could feel the unfair fight of the darkness and light. I managed to run away and get away from them once they picked another girl to torture. Wild beasts of ego and ignorance!

I can clearly feel in my broken heart that whatever is going on is a bitter beginning of a much darker era.

They released me from the prison after three days but life feels like jail now. Nothing is the same.

* * *

Days pass, the school reopens, and yes, the girls are in compulsory hijab. Nothing feels right. We are all under so much stress—tired, unhappy, scared and living in chaos.

The government bans books under many subjects. They are killing writers and reporters. They hang thoughts, words, and punctuations along with murdering freedom and peace.

It is getting dark. We hear loud noises in our neighborhood. The regime's guards are attacking the homes and the dorms in search of any anti-government literature. We cannot rip or burn our books, so we all get together to wash books in tubs of water to dissolve freedom, knowledge, and growth. We have to do it or die. This is the situation we are living in. Total terror of intelligence and liberty.

How far can they go, and how long can we fight?

I want to get out of here. This is not my home anymore. I don't have my voice. I cannot live my truth, and I am not respected. I am not even allowed to laugh and talk to my friends on the streets. The city of love has turned to a city of hate. People have changed. Our gorgeous motherland was raped by the knights of darkness, and the kingdom fell off of its throne.

It all started with the changes I saw in Ali. He changed and adjusted to the system, but I am certain that I do not want to change. I have to get out of here soon.

This is me, a free woman, a freedom lover, not a fighter. I am a young woman who believes in the expression of thoughts and emotions through poetry, music, books, and paintings. I don't do well with students pointing guns at students. I don't do well wearing dark clothes and locking my hair and my spirit in prison. I don't listen to the darkness. I serve the light in all. I want to get out of here. And I want to get out now.

As the Tao Te Ching says, "When you know enough is enough, it is enough to know."

11

India

Life is a miracle; believe in it.

I want to escape to India, but what about Raz? He does not want to leave his parents. He wants to stay in Iran.

I don't want to leave without him. We decide to finish school with all the ups and downs, manage it somehow, and get married. Plus, my parents don't give up on the idea of me getting a degree first, even in this disturbing time.

Laws are changing rapidly. We wake up every day to a new set of ridiculous laws.

Ayatollah Khomeini announces, "We do not want engineer women." How about that? Women can become doctors, nurses, and school teachers, but not engineers! Okay, what now?

The school is closed again due to demonstrations and daily protests. I am looking for a job to work with a dentist and figure out if I want to study dentistry or not. They play with people's lives. We cannot even choose our profession. I am suffocating here. God, get me out of this mess. I cannot stand it anymore.

I get a job at a dentist's office in a fancy location in Tehran, close to my home. I miss Dr. Amir, my music teacher at the university. Life is a struggle now even more than before. He made the obstacles disappear, at least for an hour imagining a peaceful world.

Hey, let's imagine. It's an appropriate time for John Lennon's sweet and inspiring song:

Imagine all the people
sharing all the world

47

You may say that I'm a dreamer
but I'm not the only one
I hope someday you'll join us
and the world will live as one"

Imagination is the blueprint of life's coming attractions. I miss the safe cocoon we used to build to rest in while playing music together. Where is Dr. Amir now when my spirit yearns for his light and wisdom?

* * *

For eight-hour-long and never-ending days, in absolute boredom, I watch the dentist go in and out of panicked people's mouth. They are in such fear from the very first moment they sit on that frightening black leather chair with eye-piercing lights. No number of love songs playing in the background or soothing sounds of bubbling water in the aquarium can cease their anxiety. Even the fish don't look peaceful here. They also feel the tension in the aura of this well-decorated room. The air smells of medicines and carries a thick cloud of fear.

Do I want to work in this energy? Can I manage? Will I get used to this?

Oh God, I don't like this scenario at all. I won't be a good dentist like Dr. Hamid. He is a young man who loves his work. He enjoys his time reading books about teeth and loves spending time with our patients. I don't. This is not for me. I won't be honest to myself, my profession, or my patients. Surely it is not authentic to work just to make a living. There must be another way, and I am determined to find it soon.

The day came when honest words flew out of my mouth on autopilot while I was holding the rubber suction in my hand, hearing the irritating sound it makes, dreaming of my future in bright hues, and collecting saliva from a patient's mouth. Oh yes, the magic suction did it. With no control over my words, my spirit took over and said what it had to say loud and clear. In that moment, I became the most powerful creator of my own destiny.

Once the truth was expressed so spontaneously, I transformed into a proud witness of my righteousness. I did not stop myself saying, "Dr. Hamid, I want to go to India. I have made my decision. I am going. I quit pretending and lying to myself. I quit ignoring my wishes. I am so ready to abandon the fear of the unknown. Please find another assistant, because I will be leaving soon."

I feel great saying these words. A heavy weight lifts off my chest. I speak with confidence and from the point of power. This is my life, and I am in charge. I am creating my world, and I decide for myself.

The patient, with his mouth fully open, is saying something that neither one of us can understand. He signals for me to wait.

Okay, I'll wait. I am not sure what is he going to suggest. I am waiting impatiently. Is he going to tell me something about India? I cannot wait.

After his treatment, he begins talking about India and the complications a young woman can face being alone there.

"You need a guide," he says. "Someone to help you find a place to live and help you to get enrolled into a university." He talks about the differences in our cultures, food, values, and so much more.

"How do you know all this, Mr. K.?" I ask.

"I do business with India, and I have a business partner who visits Iran once a year," he replied. "I will introduce you to him to help you there. Please wait to meet him and then decide."

Talk about karma! We have many patients coming and going daily, and my big mouth has to open during his visit. What is cooking? I am not sure. All I know is that we plan and God laughs.

"Okay," I respond, and I thank him for his thoughtful offer.

* * *

"Raz, I cannot tolerate this regime and their nonsense anymore," I tell him. "I am choking here. I must leave. This is a national prison. I have to hide who I am. My opinions are worthless, and my life is insignificant. I cannot even read a book that I like, and I have to wear something that is not me. I have decided to leave. I want to leave as soon as I graduate."

Then I ask, "Do you want to go with me to India, Raz?"

"No," he says. "I cannot. I must stay here with my parents. Plus, I don't want to live in India."

We both cry hard, in total confusion and pain.

He suggests we get engaged and forget about the new regime. If we are together, everything will be fine. "You will get used to this lifestyle, I promise you," he assures me. "Just like everyone else. We will be like many other people living here."

Part of me agrees with him, and a whole other part of me screams *no*.

"This way of living has nothing to do with our engagement," I cry. "The government is not going to change if I wear an engagement ring."

"Oh, of course, everything is going to be different," he reassures me.

"In what way, Raz? Don't you see what is going on here?"

* * *

At times, in my silence, my confused and crazy brain lectures my heavy heart, and this is what I hear: *Raz can solve your problems. He always repairs everything. Remember the day the vacuum cleaner broke and he fixed it? The other day, he even repaired the washing machine for Mom. Give your frustration with the government to him, and he will take care of it. He is your hero! A man who can fix a machine can also fix your life!*

Yes, of course, the engagement ring is the answer to all of my personal, social, and political problems. My brain wins at last. It is not so smart, but it is stubborn enough to win the argument—just like an annoying but persistent salesman who sells you something you absolutely do not need and do not care for by convincing you that you have to have it and you need to have it *now*. This is my situation.

"Tell your family that I will come on Friday with my parents for a visit, and we will get engaged as soon as possible. Actually, I will bring the engagement ring," Raz tells me with such joy.

Okay, Raz, let's do it, and all will be fixed! Sooner the better. The diamond ring will solve our political and social issues instantaneously, and we will live happily ever after. Wow, that was such a quick fix! Why did I not think of it sooner?

The magic ring is coming to change my life. It will bring me freedom of choice and liberty of soul. What else could I want?

"Mom, Dad, Raz is coming on Friday with his family to talk about our engagement."

Great, awesome! Laughter and joy fills my home again. We all love Raz. My family believes that he can certainly fix my world, and ultimately, I will forget about India and freedom!

* * *

It is Friday. *The* Friday. The ring is on its way to mend my life, to manifest my dreams, and to change my world completely, undoubtedly, and magically. I am pacing in my room, as if I am on a mission. Preparation is going on in the kitchen. Delicious pastries, appetizers, and dinner are being arranged for Raz, my soon-to-be fiancé, and his family.

I have rollers in my hair and a dried-up beauty mask on my face. I walk aimlessly; my legs feel like jelly and my brain looks like a teenager's room—messy, cluttered, confused, and chaotic. Nothing is in order. Nothing matches but my nail polish and my lipstick. Isn't that enough for a happy life? What else do I want?

My heart is protesting. I can hear the slogans in my ears loud and strong: *Don't do it. Take control of your life. Go and explore. Leave and live. You cannot find happiness here. Raz cannot fix your world, though he is great at fixing vacuum cleaners and washing machines. Only you can create your own reality. Making you happy and fixing your world is not his responsibility. You are responsible for every possibility in your life. You can do it. Stand up and find your place in the world.*

My poor heart beats so fast, screaming, *Say yes to me! Trust me and follow me! Do not listen to your confused brain. Listen to me, feel me, hear me, and run for your life! Find the magic key to unlock happiness.*

I run out of my bedroom to the living room, which has been decorated with candles, gorgeous fresh flowers, and all kinds of goodies on the coffee table. I am breathless. My chest is tight, and my knees cannot tolerate my weight. I am shaking with anxiety.

My mom looks at me with two big question marks in her eyes. "What is going on now?" she asks. 'Why aren't you ready? They are arriving any minute."

She does not want to give me a chance to explain myself. All she is wishing for in this moment is an obedient, well-trained, compliant daughter. She does not want me, who always has an opinion about living. She wants me to be quiet and not have an idea about how I want to live my life. At least now, today. *Please God, no more discussions about life. Make her get dressed and be quiet for once ... please God ... and for sure, no India anymore!* I can hear the chatter in Mom's brain and feel the fear in her breath.

I hold her hands and beg her to be quiet for a moment. I want her to look into my eyes, find me, feel me, and listen to me.

My tears are running over the dried-up face mask making lines on my face. My tears are painting the path for me. They are drawing the track to my future. The lines are changing with each stream of tears, showing me the impermanence of everyday life. My tears are teaching me about the importance of flow and movement. They are comforting me by releasing the heartache, the anguish, and the sorrow from my chest. They kindly and gently wash away my commitment to despair. They are clearing the trail for me, encouraging me to keep walking toward freedom—freedom of self!

"Mom, please, go downstairs and tell them I cannot do it. I cannot look into Raz's eyes. Our love for each other makes me weak. Please ask him to go home and do not contact me. I love him, but I have to go. I want to go. I cannot do it. I cannot get engaged and expect him to make me happy. I must find happiness on my own."

My mom is furious. "Why are you so difficult? Why aren't you like all other girls? What is wrong with you? What more do you want? You are lucky to have Raz in your life. You will never find another man as good as him. I cannot understand you, girl. You will ruin your future with all the unnecessary noise you create in your mind."

"Mom, you might be right," I admit. "I might never find anyone like him in my life. But I am ready to take a chance. I must leave this country. This is unbearable for me. I cannot be happy living in unrealistic boundaries and restrictions. I must go and allow my wishes to manifest. I want to live totally, freely, and passionately. Being alive only is not an option for me!"

I continue, "I understand that you are disappointed. I know you want an obedient daughter, but my soul is of a different nature. I am here to live my message, and being in this golden cage does not allow me to live my purpose. I have wings. Let me fly!"

She is hearing me but not listening to me. I see the confusion in her face and the sadness in her eyes. She lost her daughter in that moment.

They are here. The bell is singing a cheerful song. My home is celebrating my honesty. Flowers are proud of me, sitting in their crystal vases. The flame in the candle cannot stop dancing.

I leave the room when my mom answers the doorbell.

My body is shaking. My heart is racing. My tears are running, but my spirit is dancing to the music of freedom, I am growing wings on my back. I can fly. Finally, the chains are broken, and I speak my truth. I not only choose freedom for me but release Raz from the chains of my selfishness. Now he is responsible for his own happiness and does not have to work so hard to make me happy. I must first be joyful in order to share my happiness with another person. It is unforgivable to think my happiness must become someone else's chore.

We are both free. Dear future, here we come.

We break up. The destiny, the inescapable law of karma, and our stories push us in two different directions. We part ways to find ourselves.

And Mom was absolutely right. I never found another man as kind, truthful, and romantic as Raz. He was the one and only—my first love, pure and true. He signed up for all of it, and I carry him in my heart forever.

No one loved me the way you did, my dear Raz. I wish you happiness always and in all ways, my love.

* * *

Now take a deep breath and listen to the rest of my story. Life is full of unexpected and sudden sharp turns, and only when we allow the flow in every turn do we face magic and miracles.

Unplanned, unforeseen, surprising, days pass. The phone is ringing. Mom shouts from the other room, "Answer the phone."

I run to the phone. "Good morning, Kangarloo's residence," I say politely.

"Hi, Miss Kathy, this is K., your patient from Dr. Hamid's clinic."

"Oh, hello, how are you?"

"Fine," he replies. "Just wanted to let you know that Mr. B. Singh, my friend from India, is visiting Tehran at this time. Would you like to meet him and get the information you need about the university and living in India?"

The voices of my parents echo in my brain, insisting that I meet this man before embarking on this journey. They firmly believe that to know someone local in India is important. We still don't know when I will leave, but I know in my heart that it will happen soon. Remember? I am weird, I hear voices!

"Sure, Mr. K. I appreciate your kindness so much. Can you please give me his phone number?"

And here we go. The hand of destiny is now holding my hand, leading me to my next chapter, unknowingly and unexpectedly.

I call Mr. Singh's hotel and go to meet him for lunch, taking my nosy younger sister with me. He is a gentleman, willing to help and very open about sharing all that he knows with us. He gives me many helpful hints about India and promises to help me as one of his family members once I arrive.

I am very pleased with this meeting. Now I have more confidence to choose the date and plan my visit. I thank him and invite him to have dinner with my family at my home before he leaves, and he accepts the invitation graciously.

*　*　*

Days pass, and I am still debating whether to make my wish a reality. Ifs, whats and hows are screaming in my mind, messing up the tranquility of my aura.

Meanwhile, the pressure is building up on women. We are devastated. We do not want to wear a uniform and cover our hair. Most importantly, we want to pursue the profession we desire. We must stand up for our rights. I am confident we can do something about it.

An organization of independent women announces a demonstration against hijab. They ask all the participants to wear black outfits to show the depression we are going through. Black in Iran is a sign of mourning, and of course we are mourning the death of individual freedom for women.

I am super-energized today. We are going to do it, and the world will hear our voice. It is time.

I wear a light gray shirt and blue jeans, not paying attention to the dress code and totally unaware of the divine plan. Here I go to participate in the most important event of my life, unaware of the depth and importance of this happening.

Women are gathered in thousands, all in black. Some even wear short veils as a sign of grief and sorrow. We have a peaceful march bursting with positive energy. The slogans are about respect and freedom for all. Reporters from many TV stations, newspapers, and magazines are covering the walk. We, the women, are proud of it. This gathering will have a positive effect not only on Iranian women but for all other women bound by barbaric laws and rules. We deserve to choose freely and live in freedom.

That is the least one can ask for.

* * *

My mom's best friend calls our home early the next morning in total shock. Her voice is trembling. "Did you see the morning newspapers?"

"No," my mom replies. "Is everything okay?"

"Kathy's full-page picture is on the cover of all morning newspapers with a red X on it. They are searching for her. The government wants to arrest her. She is in danger—hide her. They are dangerous. They are killing people for no reason."

The eye of a camera randomly chose me among thousands of women participants. That could be because of the color of my clothes. Just because I was not in black, the camera captured me. As simple as that. This incident was enough for the government to arrest me and kill me to teach the women of Iran a lesson. They want us to listen, not question, and blindly follow the rules.

We are stunned. No one talks. The air is heavy. Walls are crushing me. What is the way out?

"Do you still want to go to India?" Dad asks in panic.

"Yes!" I scream.

"Now?"

"Yes."

"Are you ready?"

"I can get ready."

"Let's arrange for your new passport and get you a visa to India."

My dad knows many people; he has influential connections. My new passport is ready in a day, and a young man named Anand is helping to get my visa. The word *Anand* means happiness in Hindi. How true! He becomes the source of bliss for me.

* * *

I call Mr. B. Singh in New Delhi to tell him about my plan. He is going to receive me at the Delhi airport. Everything is planned according to the divine will. Who are we? When the time is right, the universe opens the door. Sometimes you walk voluntarily through the open gates, and other times you are pushed through a crack. It all depends on time and purpose. We are offered a path according to our soul-contract. We must be ready to see the open door and walk through it with least resistance.

My family is comforted by the fact that I have someone in India to help me and to guide me. I am not even a bit worried. I am too excited to be worried. I just feel weird—so strange. There is a feeling that I cannot explain. This is what I was waiting for all my life. I am dying to go, but what about my friends, my mom, dad, sister, brother? How can I not see my grandma every day? Wow. So tough.

I must leave everything and everyone behind. I am nervous and anxious, but at the same time excited to my core. Such a mix of emotions. One minute I am angry at the newspaper and the result of the demonstration, the next moment I am filled with gratitude for all that occurred. I have an inexplicable feeling of accepting the most unusual situation. There is no way to explain such a mix; you understand it once you experience it. Words are too limited to take you there. It is shocking and exhilarating at the same time. I am a cocktail of emotions.

* * *

It is October 28, 1983, to be exact. Time to fly to India. In four hours, I will land in New Delhi.

I am sure you can imagine the fusion of emotions erupting in me while on the flight. I always wanted to go to India, but not in such a rush and fear. The universe is your secretary; its job is to fulfill your heartfelt wishes. How this wise secretary is planning the road to manifestation is unknown to even the most awakened mystic.

I arrive, but after going through immigration, I realize that my bag did not get there. My luggage did not make it to Delhi. It is lost in Bombay.

I am in India without my luggage, with only $500 (the amount we are allowed to get out of Iran), a one-way ticket, my picture on the front page of a few newspapers, and twenty-three years of memories.

I left my home, my love, my family, and my past behind to explore a total unknown future by myself. The world is my playground, and I am ready to play.

Mr. B. Singh is at the airport to receive me. He is very kind. I am quiet in the car, trying to hide my emotions. I cannot talk much. Talking makes me cry.

We reach the hotel. He checks me in and follows me to my room to make sure I am comfortable and safe. I trust him immensely, and without hesitation, I hand him my passport, my money, and my ticket before he leaves. I do not think twice about "what if." It is all about "what is" at this point. He is now my family, my friend, and all that I have in India, so I trust him.

"Rest well, and in the morning, I will send a driver to pick you up and take you to my home," he says.

I am excited, but I don't even have clean clothes or a toothbrush. He asks me not to worry. Everything will be fine.

"Our home is close to the marketplace," he tells me. "When you get there, my sister-in-law will take you shopping. Okay?"

"All right. Thank you," I say in full gratitude.

I lock my door, take a shower, and go to bed. The clean white starched sheets with the smell of fresh soap hug me so tight. I am happy. I giggle. I am where I am supposed to be. I am in India! Oh no, I am home at last.

I am free! I can breathe. I am overjoyed.

I sleep like a newborn baby. I have cracked the hardened eggshell that was my home for twenty-three years, stretched my wings, and got out of Iran. I stretched some more on the plane and stepped on the broken pieces of the eggshell that was for a long time my shelter. I am not restricted anymore. I can fly.

Namaste, India. Hello, life!

A sense of peacefulness adds to the aroma of India. The noisy streets and the faded chants from the close-by temple in the background tell me I am home. I have finally arrived, and there is no looking back.

Go forward, Kathy. The world is yours.

* * *

At seven in the morning, I hear a knock on the door.

"Yes?"

"Room service, ma'am."

I did not order anything, I think to myself. I open the door and see a nice breakfast tray.

"Mr. B. Singh just called and ordered you breakfast," says the waiter.

"Oh, thank you!"

The boy places the tray on the little round table by the window. The hazy sky of New Delhi calls me: *Eat, get ready, and begin your new life.* The whole world seems to be excited for me.

A cup of freshly brewed tea and a slice of warm toast with butter and honey fill every cell of my body with gratitude.

* * *

The driver arrives at eleven. I am ready. He is polite and quite shy. He does not make eye contact and only answers me with "Yes ma'am" and "No ma'am."

I have thousands of questions while driving. I just cannot shut up! I am on life's strongest steroid. I want to know everything about India in that thirty-minute drive.

The loud streets are filled with vendors, buses, and cars; carts pulled by horses, bulls, or camels; bicycles and motorcycles; rickshaws, three-wheelers, and scooters; dogs and sacred cows. They are all moving in a strange non-rhythmic rhythm together. *The only thing missing in the chaos is an airplane in the middle of the road*, I think to myself and laugh in ultimate joy.

I find the rhythm—a very special tempo in the midst of this chaos. Life goes orderly in the presence of such disorder. It is hard to describe.

After about half an hour of live entertainment by the amusing tangled traffic, we arrive at the house. This is a home of a joint family. This home belongs to three brothers. They live here with their wives, their mother, and six kids. Each brother has two kids. The father made his transition a few years ago.

Everything looks perfect. A family of thirteen people.

I meet everyone, go to the bazaar, and buy a few things to wear. We have a delicious lunch. After our meal, Mr. B. Singh's mother, who is the head of the family, asks me if I want to see a little apartment they have close by—if I want to live near them and have my own little place. I say sure. What else do I want? I already have a family here.

We all walk to the property, which is going through a major remodeling. A part of this building was not touched, and they offer it to me rent-free. I say yes, and I ask permission to help them in exchange with typing, shipping, receiving, and things like that in their office. They accept my offer graciously.

Now I have one little room with a tiny kitchenette and a bathroom. I am so happy to be so lucky.

We walk back to their home, and by the time we finish our delicious dinner, my room is set. I move in the same night.

I have two shirts, two pairs of pants, a toothbrush, and a few other pieces of necessary toiletry. It is enough, because I am where I always wanted to be. Nothing matters at this point, and I love it!

* * *

The next day, I go to the United Nations office with a cut-out of the newspaper in my hand. I show the officer the photograph, go through an interview, and become a refugee of the United Nations.

Another sharp turn in my life has changed my path. No visits to Iran. All gone. No more family. No more grandmother, aunts, cousins, mom, dad, sister, or brother around, at least for a while—until they can come to see me in India.

Everything I have ever known is gone overnight. This is proof of the impermanence of life. Some things we cannot predict, and when they happen, there is no way of changing them. The only option is to accept the new, bless the past, and move on.

This is exactly what I do.

You wanted India that bad? That demonstration, the photographer, morning newspapers, and the photograph were merely instruments to take me where I wanted to be. They helped me to manifest my dream. They became my ticket to freedom. Sometimes blessings wrap themselves in unattractive masks to make sure we are serious about welcoming them into our lives.

I believe at the end of each tunnel, there is a bright flashing neon sign saying, "Well done! You are a hero!"

* * *

I help the Singh brothers at the office. They have an international import/export company.

I notice B. Singh is quite sad. "Are you okay?" I ask.

"No," he says. "My marriage is falling apart."

"Why?"

"My wife and I cannot get along. It has been the same since we got married. We do not understand each other."

This makes me sad. Thinking of a young family falling apart just like my childhood story and the story of the goose.

"You must work on it. Can I help? I can talk to her," I suggest.

I try to play the role of marriage counselor in their unhappy life, using my own life experiences with my parents. I talk with his wife for hours at a time, but things do not look good. She just wants to leave. Her mind is set.

B. Singh and I become close friends. He opens up to me, and I become his secret-keeper. His wife does not like it. She does not like anything. She is done with the marriage, already checked out. One day, she takes the kids, leaves the family home, and moves in with her parents. She is gone.

B. Singh and the whole family follow her. He begs her to come back for the sake of the children: twin boys, only two years old at the time. But the bridge is broken, and she refuses to come back. Their chapter is shut, closed. She has made her decision. Her family and the laws of India back her up. She does not want to live in the family home and wants to exit the marriage. It is the official end of a ten-year estrangement.

* * *

I stay at my little apartment and work at the office. B. Singh and I grow closer through hours of talking, lunches, dinners, and secrets shared. We begin to know and trust each other. We like to be together. It feels sweet.

One early morning, about five o'clock, the doorman of the building knocks at my door.

"Yes?" I answer.

"Ma'am, sir is here."

"Sir? Who sir?"

"Mr. B. Singh."

"Okay, let me get dressed. I am coming."

I am worried. What could have happened? It is still dark outside. Why is he here? I put on my robe and open the door.

He is standing there dressed tastefully in a light gray/bluish suit with a light blue turban. He looks as if he is on the most important mission of his life.

"Please come in," I say. "It is very early in the morning. Is everything okay?"

"Yes, it is all fine."

"Please, sit."

He is standing by the door, uncertain of something totally unclear to me. I am looking at him not understanding what is going on.

All of a sudden, I feel a shift in his field of energy. He centers himself. Directly looking into my eyes, and with the confidence of a superhero from a blockbuster romantic Bollywood movie, he says, "Will you marry me?"

"Who?" I look around the room, seeing no one.

"You, Kathy."

"Are you okay, Banka?"

"Yes. I am very much okay. Please, will you marry me?"

I pause for a second. Sit on a chair. Clear my throat, looking through him as if he does not exist. I am totally out of my body.

And I say yes.

I have no idea what happened in that moment of that day. I just said yes. Half asleep, half shocked, a bit awake, I answered yes.

We both sit in surprise, looking at each other. Was he even awake when he made this decision? It is five in the morning, for God's sake. Somebody, anybody, tell us what is going on.

The more I think about my answer, though, the more I feel at ease.

"Get dressed. Let's go to my mother. She is waiting to bless us at home."

"Wow! She knows that you are here?" I ask.

"Yes. We were talking all night about you. She is waiting for us."

This is more intense than Bollywood. My God, what is happening?

"Give me few minutes to get ready," I ask. What to wear? How to get dressed? What are we doing? Is this real?

Finally, I get ready, and we are on our way to pick up what we have left in our past lives. Destiny and the law of karma brought a twenty-three-year-old woman and a twenty-eight-year-old man form different parts of this world together to create a sweet love story in such awesomeness. Our union feels innocent and real.

We run to his mother, who is waiting at home to hear the good news. We are excited but shy at the same time. When we enter the room, her face lights up. We embrace and share our happiness through tears and laughter. This is a beautiful moment—a day I will never forget, not planned but totally spontaneous and true. Love has its own strange way of coming into our heart.

She takes a beautiful gold bangle from her closet, hands it to me, and asks me to wear it. "This is a bracelet my mother-in-law gave me when I got engaged to Banka's dad, and it is very dear to me," she says with tears in her kind eyes. "Now it is yours. I am so happy for both of you."

I thank her and touch her feet in respect to receive blessings.

"Get out of India and get married," she says. "Do not stay here, because you are not born into a Sikh family, and this is going to be tough for many to accept. After you get married, I will announce it to the family. Go and start your life together, and do not worry about anything here. I will manage."

Banka has businesses in Germany, England, and the United States. Soon, we are on our way to Germany. We get married at a Sikh temple in Frankfurt with his mother's blessings, just the two of us. No guests, no photographer, no wedding planner, and no fuss, just a whole lot of love and caring from that day onward.

* * *

That was the start of twenty-two years of marriage, two wonderful kids, so many precious memories, and much to be thankful for, just because I said yes at five in the morning, half asleep, half unconscious, but fully orchestrated by the law of karma.

I said yes to twenty-two years of learning, sharing, traveling, love, and happiness. But like many other relationships, ours had a fairy-tale beginning and a painful ending. Eleven years after our marriage, we moved to Dubai, and that was the end of our blissful marriage and the beginning of the breaking of our nest. My husband got interested in gambling with a few other friends. This was something that I did not like, approve of, or even understood. Yet I stayed fully committed to our marriage for the sake of my kids.

In the year 2007, after my daughter graduated from university and my son completed high school, I exited the marriage. It had been a colorful mix of blessings and painful lessons that changed my perspective and the way I viewed life. I learned, shared, grew, and moved forward. I have never had any regret about saying yes when he proposed.

I am a believer in divine timing, divine order, and the law of karma. We came together at the right time. Our hearts recognized each other, and our union became a safe sanctuary of our spirits. I gave him unconditional love and a happy home that he'd never had. With him, I searched and explored many of my past lives in India. I was born in Iran, but my soul grew in India. And moreover, we both paid our dues and cleared our karma with each other.

I finally understood the reason of my love for India. I am writing these pages sitting in an Ayurveda center in Kerala, India, at this very moment, feeling totally at home and in my element, centered, grounded, and in love with all that is. It is November 2018.

So thank you, Banka, for taking me on the roller coaster of life, making me experience sharp turns, steep slopes, and sometime even inversions. Thank you for sharing the ride with me. I am eternally grateful for our reunion. Hoping you feel the same.

12

You Are My Project

Life is a chance: take it.

Take a deep breath before reading this story of mine, so unusual and ultimately thought-provoking in its own unique way! And here we go.

Every time I heard, "Sweetheart, you are my project," it felt like a cold, cruel death sentence. Every word of this statement shot my spirit in the heart.

I am not even sure how to begin this story. I am a strong believer in the hidden messages in various events and people we get involved with along the path. But this one is so out of the ordinary that I am not sure about the learning veiled in it. I know, however, that there are no coincidences, and each and every person in our lives has a prophecy.

I leave it up to you to find the messages and the blessings in this special episode of my life, since I am still puzzled by the complexity of the situation.

Let me walk you through the most astonishing story of my life.

* * *

When my divorce from Banka was finalized, it still took him six months to leave the family home. He was clueless about living by himself. I stayed extremely patient and compassionate with him as he gathered strength and confidence to face the reality of a broken nest for the second time in his life.

I am trying my best to understand him but in exchange, he grows angrier and bitter day by day. The fire of resentment consumes our peace and love for each other. Changes are unbearable. My body is sick, my mind is tired and my spirit is suffering the loss of peace and tranquility. I am in a hospital bed after a very unkind argument. My body cannot take it anymore. I have severe pain in my chest and my left arm. This is a sign, a powerful signal, that enough is enough. It is time to ask him to leave.

I call him from the hospital and ask him to move out as soon as possible. The relationship is undeniably toxic, and there is no room for repair, at least at this time. Neither one of us deserves this pain and misery.

I am unable to work for a few weeks. I immerse myself in yoga, meditation, and ancient Sanskrit chants for hours every day. I ask the energy of Lord Ganesha to remove all obstacles, cry to Lord Shiva to bring back the light into my life, and ask Quan Yin to give me the power and the generosity to forgive Banka in order to move forward. I need to embody the powerful energy of Mother Durga and Kali to pass through the dense and unkind energy of anger in order to find love and compassion later in life. I have a lot of work to do.

I sit for days in silence and surrender to the lord of love, Krishna. Chanting Hari Krishna is a perfect reminder of the awesomeness of Govinda Restaurant, the birthplace of my spiritual self. I do not know what else to do. My practice is my sanctuary. I stay in silence, pray long hours, and surrender to the entities of light for healing. I need to regain my strength and peace of mind, and it is not an easy task.

The knot is tight, and the lessons are buried. It feels like nothing is working. I begin searching and think that I can access the heart of the devastation in a past-life regression session. So I call the best therapist I know and make an appointment.

I am sure that I can get to the core of this heartache, release the pain, and mend my broken heart in this session. I do it all the time for others, and now it is my turn.

I get a great night's sleep, wake up early in the morning, take a relaxing shower, dress in white, eat a wholesome breakfast, and feel ready to explore one of my past lives that has the most value for me at this time in my present re-embodiment. I arrive early enough to feel the energy of Dr. Will's tranquil office and connect to the elements here.

* * *

I am in the room with Dr. Will. He is amazing in the field of past-life regression and confident that we can get to the root cause, bring it to the surface, learn the lessons, and release the pain.

The sofa I am lying on is very comfortable, and the music is soothing. Dr. Will talks in a calming tone of voice and carries compassionate energy in his aura. I feel safe and at ease here. He takes me deeper and deeper by using the same technique as I do—progressive relaxation—and my whole body feels loose and limp. My mind is clear, and my breath is very calm and slow. I have nothing to do and nowhere to go. I am staying in the moment.

His voice guides me to go deeper and deeper—down, down, down. I must trust the images and follow his voice to take me where I need to go.

We are going back on my timeline to childhood, infancy, in the womb, and even further to one of my past lives. He takes me through tunnels and back to the light. And this is what I see, clear as an Oscar-winning Hollywood movie: I am an Indian spiritual healer. I am a man dressed in white, very peaceful and kind and totally dedicated to my craft, around forty-five years of age. My name is Raja. The year is around 1920.

This may be my very recent past life. It surely can be the very last life I had before this one. Interesting!

Let me take you through my past life regression session step by step.

* * *

I see myself in a small cottage—a modest, simple setting. I am sitting on a white sofa looking out the window into the woods. I am calm and peaceful, holding a mala bead in between my fingers chanting a mantra.

And the phone rings. I answer it and hear, "Namaste, Raja. This is Gita."

"Namaste, Gita. How are you? What a surprise."

Gita is a client, not very close to me. I see her maybe once a year for healing.

"Raja, I need you to help my daughter. She sounds worried and overwhelmed."

"What is going on?" I ask, and she begins to cry. I pause to allow her to calm down, and she continues.

"A few days ago, she went to the doctor. Her blood pressure is unusually high. And after a few tests, the doctor told her the arteries to her heart are 90 percent blocked. I want her to see you. I feel strongly that you are the only person who can help her. Doctors gave up on her. I am sure you can heal her."

"How old is she?" I ask.

"Forty-seven."

"So young for such a massive problem."

"Yes, but she has it in her dad's family. My dear husband died of a sudden heart attack at the age of forty," Gita added in tears. "I am scared. Please help her, Raja."

"Oh no! I am sorry," I say. "What is your daughter's name?"

"Priya."

"Okay, please give her my number. Let me see what I can do. I will do my best. I promise."

Connecting with Priya seems difficult. It is taking us quite a long time to connect and meet.

* * *

"Kathy, let that image pass and tell me where you are now," Dr. Will asks.

I spend my days treating people in a sacred space with a high vibration. I set up next to a pond in the garden under a stunning magnolia tree with beautiful pink flowers. An exceptional hand-crafted statue of Buddha in total bliss decorates the scene. All I can hear is the soothing sound of a river in the distance, the song of wind chimes, and the choir of birds in the trees.

"Look for Priya, did you connect with her? Is she there?" Dr. Will leads me to go forward in that life and explore my connection with Priya.

"Yes, she is here." She is beautiful, with light brown hair, wearing a long white cotton dress, lying on my healing bed. She seems exceptionally relaxed and at ease while resting on the bed, allowing her body to absorb the healing rays of the sun.

I give her healing, transferring the universal life force energy into her body, especially her heart. She is open and welcoming. Her breath is calm and comforting.

After the session, she seems pleased and optimistic. She looks puzzled a bit but at the same time open to the whole process.

She tells me the story of her father. Priya remembers walking happily to a wedding with her forty-year-old dad when he collapsed and passed in an instant. She was only thirteen. Fear of death and dying is engraved on the core of her existence. She made important life decisions based on fear. She has been living in fear always and in all ways. The monster of fear became her guide while growing up.

She is eager to continue healing treatments on a regular basis. She dreads death. Priya even practices yoga and mediates daily for the same reason—escaping the angel of death. I want her to substitute trust for fear. But she seems solid in her behavior.

The reason behind the hardening of the arteries becomes so obvious to me. She is scared, and that energy has made her behave in a rigid, unbending, inflexible, super-stiff manner. She is not open to the flow of change.

"Eat more vegetables," I suggest

"I hate vegetables," says Priya.

"Add more fruits to your diet."

"I only eat apples and oranges. I do not like other fruits."

"Have you ever tried them?"

"No," she replies

And the list goes on and on … *I don't like this, I don't like that. I don't want to do this, and I don't want to do that either.* She is a thirteen-year-old stubborn child living in a forty-seven-year-old beautiful woman's body. She froze at the tender age of thirteen.

Priya is not open to try anything. This woman is living in the smallest self-made prison, which is built and controlled by fear only. Fear of everything!

The concept of change scares her because she does not want to lose control. She does not trust the flow of life. She is paralyzed by fear. How sad!

* * *

"Let go of this scene, Kathy, and move forward in that life," Dr. Will gently guides me.

I see myself giving Priya another healing session. Once I access her field of energy, I see a sweet image of a wedding next to a beautiful waterfall. *Her marriage must play a big role in her life. I must discuss the vision with her,* I think to myself. Finally, I have found the lost piece of the puzzle. This is all about her marriage.

The session ends, and I am talking to her. "Well, I saw a wedding scene, very important in your healing," I say gently. "A significant event in your life. Do you want to talk about it?"

"I am not married," she says.

"Any plans?" I ask.

"Oh, of course not."

"The vision showed that you are going to get married soon, so be prepared!" I add jokingly.

She does not even like the idea of being married—facing another significant change. "I will inform you when I want to get married, Raja," Priya says, walking away from the river.

"At least invite me. I was the first person giving you the news of your marriage," I tease her.

We laugh, and she disappears among the trees.

* * *

"What else, Kathy? Move forward," Dr. Will leads me

We meet often for healing, and Priya begins to feel much better, more balanced and relaxed and less worried about the doctor's diagnosis.

To me, it was fear that caused the calcification of arteries. She had to let go of the image of her father's passing and give life another chance. Cleansing consciously and subconsciously is the only way to healing.

But wait a minute. Why is my past-life regression so much about her? What is going on here? My mind is out of focus for a few seconds, questioning the process.

Dr. Will feels my restlessness and gives me more hypnotic suggestions. "Go deeper and deeper to see why you are connecting with Priya. Your answer is in this past life you are exploring. Kathy, relax your body more and go deeper and deeper. Allow the pictures to come to you. Do not doubt the process. Trust your subconscious mind to lead you."

I take a deep breath and continue.

* * *

I see myself sitting with Priya. This is at the end of one of my sessions with her. She has a strange look in her eyes. I cannot translate the stare.

"Are you okay, Priya? How do you feel?" I ask

"Oh, that is you," she mumbles.

"Who?"

"I was getting married to you, Raja. You are the one in the image you saw!"

"Who? Me?" I don't know what to say. I compose myself and begin talking about connections. But she is not listening.

"It is you, I am sure. I want to marry you."

"What?"

I can see us getting closer. Little by little, the shock changed to trust, the trust steered toward friendship, and before I knew it, I was in love.

Yes. It feels great. A dream come true. She is my princess, kind and beautiful. I sign up to love her and to help her on her healing journey ahead. We can heal her wounded heart with our love!

* * *

What else Kathy? Tell me what do you see. Dr. Will guides me.

I see that I have an older sister in this life who is totally against our relationship. Her name is Esha.

"Esha, you are making me angry every time you talk about Priya."

"Raja, I am worried for you. I cannot trust her," Esha says.

"But why?"

"I don't know. Something about her I cannot trust."

Every time we talk about Priya, I end up frustrated, begging my sister to support us and be happy for me. But she is worried, and I cannot understand why.

I also see my younger brother in this life. His name is Ram. He keeps on warning me about Priya as well.

I, on the other hand, totally blind and in my own love-land, do not want to hear anything but praise. I am sure you have been there at least once in your lifetime. Everyone else sees it but you.

Priya is my princess—extremely charming and totally flawless. Most importantly, she is in love with me. Name it, she has it all. Something is broken, though, which is obvious to many, but of course I can only see what I want to see, and I do not want anyone or anything to change my self-made unreal image of Priya, soon to be my queen.

Sounds familiar, yes?

We decided to move to Goa away from the memories of the past and build our new nest. We build a beautiful home in the woods and move with all of our belongings. What else do we want? This is a fairy tale, isn't it?

Life is beautiful. Everything is awesome. See? Everyone is wrong. We are the happiest couple on the planet.

Beautiful home, amazing wife—I am in paradise.

* * *

"Go forward, Kathy. What do you see next?" I hear Dr. Will say.

We are getting married next to a running river with a small waterfall under the starry sky. Just like the image in her session.

My parents, her parents, and our friends have gathered from near and far to celebrate our new life with joy and blessings. My sister Esha, however, cannot stop crying the whole time at the wedding.

"Raja, I love you. You are my brother, and I hate to see you hurt," she cries.

"I will be okay. Please don't worry. Priya is my soul mate, and this is a match made in paradise. Don't you see it all?"

"I hope that I am wrong, but this whole thing does not feel right," Esha says over and over again.

"Don't worry. We will be fine." I hug her and kiss her to calm her down.

I look at the magical waterfall, saying to myself, *They are all wrong. This is a sign from heaven. We will be fine!*

The wedding is simple and sweet. She has her family and one friend, and I have my family and a whole lot of friends. It seems as if she does not have anyone at the wedding. They are mainly my friends and family.

A forty-seven-year-old woman has no friends to attend her wedding! But I don't have time to pay attention to the details. I am busy being lost in my own dream. The thought that none of her friends comes to our wedding does not even cross my mind. Nothing wakes me from my deep slumber. They are all busy, I am sure. Many would have loved to attend their best friend's wedding, but they must all be busy. Or they are jealous of her being so perfect. Yes, this is a much better reason to believe. She has it all, and her friends are jealous. It is easy to choose not to see the truth.

The mysterious wedding ends, and it is time to go home. It is so exciting to enter my home as her husband. A deep sense of safety fills my heart.

We are walking toward our bedroom. I open the door and see that Esha, my sister, has decorated our bedroom beautifully. She wants us to be happy. There are red rose petals everywhere, lit candles dancing with joy, a lovely fragrance of lavender … everything looks perfect, artistic, and romantic.

I shower, change, and come to bed filled with love and ready to begin the most romantic married life with the love of my life. She gets out of her wedding gown, leaves it on the floor, and sits on the bed talking about her dad.

My heart feels heavy. She is not even a bit excited to be married to me.

"By the way, what are all these candles?" Priya says. "Let me off these; they smell awful. Useless decoration! I don't like your sister, and I do not care for these."

She blows out all the candles and gets back in bed with her back toward me.

I try to fall asleep, wondering about tomorrow. My brain is the size of a pea. I cannot think. I am in a thick fog. I am lost. My heart is shrinking. I am melting, and my dream life is shattered to pieces right in front of my eyes before it even begins.

* * *

I am crying, and Dr. Will keeps on guiding me to go deeper and to see more. Do I want to see more?

I take a deep breath and continue.

Days pass. Every night, Priya brings a journal in bed to write. Either she brings a book or her journal so as not to make any physical connection with me. What happened? We just got married. She refuses to be touched and stays away so as not to touch me. There has been no physical contact from the night of our wedding.

"Priya, my love, are you okay?" I ask.

"Yes. I am just processing being married."

"Processing what?"

"Being married. I will be fine. Give me time to process."

Days and nights change turns, seasons go through their own sweet reincarnation, years pass, the gap grows wider, and the pain feels deeper in my heart. I offer her healing sessions, but she refuses to be touched even for healing. No physical or emotional intimacy passes between us. No more yoga or meditation practices either. She stops the flow of any kind of energy that could bring us closer.

What changed overnight? How did our crystal castle shatter, and where is this darkness coming from? What happened to our kisses and hugs? What just happened?

It feels as if we are in a show—a play with a bitter script. I feel like a thing, not a human being. Maybe she only wanted to show her friends and family that she could get married. I am not sure, and she refuses to talk about it.

I remember when I met her sister for the first time, she looked into my eyes and said, "You are a nice man. You seem very gentle. Why are you marrying my sister?"

I took it as a joke. I did not pay attention to this comment. I thought she was playing or maybe even she was jealous of her perfect sister. I did not see any signal because I only wanted to see what I wanted to see, and nothing could have alarmed me.

Now I know why she asked that question. But it is too late.

I feel uncomfortable in my home with her. She feels like a stranger to me—a total stranger in my bedroom, kitchen, sharing my bathroom. What is this?

* * *

"Go further, Kathy. Let the emotions go and see what is next," I hear Dr. Will's gentle voice leading me.

"I see us in the bedroom. She removes her shirt and says, 'Come feel my back.'"

"I don't feel anything. It feels normal," I say.

"Feel it here." She takes my finger and puts it on her spine.

"Feel it," she says again.

"It is a bone, isn't it?"

"No, it is a chip," she tells me.

"What chip?" I ask.

"This is a chip from aliens. They are studying me, and you are my project."

"What? I am your project?"

* * *

I am weeping, and Dr. Will is trying hard to calm me down. "Kathy this is just the past. Breathe. Pay attention. You are getting there."

I was not prepared to hear this.

What? A project?

I feel the bitter taste of dishonesty and deceit in her every word. I feel betrayed. My heart aches.

From that day on every time I complain or ask her questions about our marriage, she looks right into my eyes and says, with a cold scary smile, "You are my project, sweetheart."

This is incomprehensible. Where were these aliens, the chip in her back, and the project before our wedding? Who is this woman, and what is she doing in my home?

Now I am not comfortable. I don't feel safe, and I want to get out of here as soon as I can. But I lost my little home next to the river in the process of getting married, and I left my world in the hope of creating the most beautiful married life. Now I am a project. Life can change overnight. We read it in books, and we see it in the movies. This is for sure a blockbuster!

Staying rooted in my truth, centered in my world, and understanding how my life changed as soon as we exchanged our wedding vows is a map to follow on the foggy road to clarity. I moved from being the love of her life to an untouchable project. In the most sacred moment of a sweet beginning, the shadow of a bitter ending was present.

* * *

"Take deep breaths, Kathy. Go deeper. Look for the lesson in this. Tell me what happened next," Dr. Will asks in wonder.

I live in that scary, dark ice castle for four years, and then one day, when Priya becomes physically threatening, I decide to move back to my hometown. I leave all of my belongings, everything I have. I take my life and my dear little dog and say goodbye to my material possessions. I do not want to ever come back here again.

I am saving my soul from the claws of sorrow.

My sister and my little brother were right. They could not see exactly what was wrong, but they could feel that something was definitely not right. Esha's words echo in my mind: *This is too good to be true.* And she was right.

Priya doesn't want to reveal the reason behind our marriage. Every time I bring up the complicated issues in our marriage, she says: "What else do you want from me? I am home. I don't work. I am with you twenty-four hours a day, and I am processing being married. I told you: you are my project, my dear."

* * *

Dr. Will begins guiding me to another scene of that life. I see Priya being severely sick twice, and each time I go back to help her heal.

"Are you seeing anything else, Kathy? Go all the way to explore the teachings. Stay focused. Deeper, deeper, deeper, down down, down."

I breathe heavily. My heart is open, exploring the messages hidden in this life. It takes me a while to get clarity on the lesson I am supposed to learn from the information I have received. Somewhere in between conscious and subconscious realms lives the truth.

I take a breath, dive deep to access it, and continue.

Living with Priya is the most painful time of my life, and she is the coldest person, with no empathy toward anyone. Her body is falling apart just because of lack of compassion toward herself and others.

Oh, I see a bird. She has an old parrot. The wings of the parrot are not clipped, and the gate of the cage is always open. This bird does not know how to fly. A bird with a full set of wings has fear of flying, Every time I look at the bird, I see the similarities between the two of them. Both are prisoners of their fear.

The bird does not like anyone but her. The bird does not show any appreciation to the person feeding him. This little bird just screams, bites, and is angry for absolutely no obvious reason. They feed off of each other's energy—the same energy split into two forms, a bird and a human being.

Living in constant fear is paralyzing. It kills the spirit and murders love. They are both in a self-made jail living in the darkness of their souls, and there is nothing and nobody to help them. The door of the cage is open, the wings are intact, but the soul is in a prison built by fear. They purposely lost the key so as not to unlock happiness.

* * *

"Let the fear go in order to live! This is my lesson, Dr. Will. Raja reminded me of the value of self-love, self-confidence, and self-respect."

"Are you ready to face the world now? Do you trust that you will be protected and safe, Kathy?"

"Yes, I am. I do."

"Great, Kathy, it is time for you to come back." I hear the sweet voice of Dr. Will saying, "Take a few deep breaths. Stretch your body. Move your fingers and toes. Take another deeper breath. Open your eyes. You are back."

Yes, I am back. The sofa is wet with my tears. My eyes are shut, but my heart feels light and filled with gratitude for exploring my most complicated past life.

"Wow, Dr. Will, what was that?"

"Kathy, you did well. I know it was very emotional, but you did great! Now tell me what you felt, and more importantly, tell me what you learned from this session."

"I learned that there is no becoming. We are who we are, and that is a fact. Now I know that I cannot be responsible for changes in other people. I was reminded of my strengths and weaknesses. It brought clarity to my existence, my dharma, and my karma. Thank you, Dr. Will. I need to go home to reflect on what happened today."

* * *

Later that night, while meditating and thinking of Banka, I learn that I matter. I am a strong woman, and I can be by myself.

I learn the value of passion in a relationship. Happiness and peace must be my priority. I am proud of myself for leaving a poisonous relationship in search of freedom and happiness.

Most significantly, I learn there is no changing others; they are who they are. You either accept them or kiss them goodbye.

The challenges I faced made me strong enough to take a free fall, trusting that the net will open somewhere in the process. I am forever grateful for all the lessons I have received. Self-confidence, self-love, and self-respect can be sweet fruits of a bitter event. There was a time when I could only see the light in my heart, and the only comforting voice in my ear was the voice of God telling me this shall pass.

These monumental events taught me the importance of forgiveness and compassion. I have learned to trust life with all its ups and downs. I erase doubt from my dictionary. Hope became my companion, my friend, and my confidant.

Most importantly, I have learned to say no to abuse and disrespect. I have learned that a good wife is not an abused wife. I recognize my self-worth and become aware of the value of self-respect. It has taken me a while, but I learn it anyway. Yes, I am a yogi—or better to say, I am yoga and not a yoga mat! These dark days can count as blessings only if I learn from them.

Life does not happen in the pages of a book but in connections. Life is the greatest guru of all. It teaches me through hands-on happenings and daily experiences. It is present in my tears and my laughter. Every experience is saved in the memory bank of each cell of my body. My lessons determine who I am. I navigate my life through the narrow back alleys of my stories. Life does not happen to me; I must make it happen.

Every handshake, kiss, and hug is registered to shape our incredibly unique existence. We are one with the people we meet and we connect to.

We are not separated from our involvements and the events in our lives. We are one whole package, one whole bundle of vibration and emotions.

Positive or negative feelings with high or low vibes paint the picture of who we really are. These are the elements forming our conscious, subconscious, and super-conscious minds. They decide where we are heading. What we feel in our heart and how we see our world draw the map of our journey. We are one with the world around us and all that we experience.

People are merely guides walking us on our unique paths. They are our road signs. They create circumstances for us to feel, to respond, and to choose the path we want to be ours. They are distinguished elements of growth and change.

Think about it. Go deeper and feel the feelings of an old relationship, one which is gone already. Connect the dots to see the map it created for you. You would not be here now if it was not for the happenings of that experience. The knowledge becomes part of you embedded in the truth of who you are now in this very second.

The moment you begin thinking of your life in this manner and see everything and everyone as cheerleaders for your spiritual growth, you will stop holding grudges in your heart or being unforgiving or unkind. Your vision will change drastically when you take responsibility for all of your choices in life. You will open the gate of blessings into your life when you accept the fact that people appear on your path based on the law of karma and the exchange of energy between souls.

Karma brings us together. This is a part we have no control over, but we as part of the collective intelligence governing the cosmos are in total control to say yes or no based on free will. Karma and free will go hand in hand. Our present experiences create our future karma while we are living our past karma in this very moment.

Think deeper and see your role in all the episodes of your life. By understanding the importance of karma and free will, you move from being a victim to a master. You write the script, you direct the play, you have the power to choose who is in your life, and you play the role. You and I are in charge of all endeavors, good, bad, or indifferent.

We do create our lives with everyone, everything, and every event. For a moment, stop blaming others, events, or situations. Instead, see yourself as the conductor. You wrote the music that is now playing, so listen carefully and learn how to dance.

Every step you take leads you to create the next step in this complex dance. Every stroke of the brush on this canvas brings you closer to creating the image you desire to portray. So be awake and take watchful steps and mindful strokes, because once it is done, there is no coming back. Live it and learn from it. Be brave and truthful and say to yourself: yes, I did it.

All beings appeared in my life to play a vital role. I take full responsibility for the decisions I made accordingly. After all, life is an unchoreographed dance. We move spontaneously. We take steps according to our understanding. One step forward, one step back. I danced in my marriage, but I chose to leave once the energy seemed to be stuck and there was no flow. I learned my lessons and hope the other people involved learned theirs.

People live their lives blaming others, the world, the weather, the traffic, the food, the job, the marriage, and so forth and so on. This way, life gets miserably easy! They are miserable, but it is easy to blame others.

Another group believes in free will and takes responsibility for all risks and results. Being in a miserable marriage, a horrible job, an unhealthy body, or a loveless relationship is a choice. Living a healthy lifestyle, in a loving relationship with the self and others, is also a choice.

What did I learn?

"I have a choice, and I choose happiness!"

13

Perfect Now

Life is a book: write it.

Time to put the past behind and come to the now.

Surprisingly, I have been living in Southern California for the last nine years. I did not move to another city or a different continent for a change. Hard to believe. Finally, I found the place I love to call home.

I have full days of work and play. This is how my day unfolds: I wake up around six in the morning. I have a simple breakfast, which includes a banana, an apple, and few pieces of papaya with almond butter. I also make myself a cup of delicious hot and spicy chai with cinnamon, cardamom, ginger, turmeric, and homemade almond milk. My chai is very famous among friends and family, by the way. I enjoy every bite and savor every sip.

After breakfast, I go to the gym and the pool to swim, exercise, and lose myself to the movements of yoga or dance for two hours. My work begins at ten in the morning with either a private reiki session, past-life regression, or future-life progression, depending on my appointments. I take a peaceful lunch break in the middle of the day, eating homemade, simple, fresh meals. I end my work day teaching yoga and meditation classes in the evening.

Two days a week, I teach Yukt yoga to celebrate the deep connection of our physical body with the spirit. Other evenings, Om chanting and Tao Te Ching lead us to the land of love, wisdom, silence, and peace.

Dinner is usually a bowl of salad and fruit with nuts and a cup of hot and relaxing chamomile tea while watching comedy or something inspirational. I haven't had cable TV for the last fifteen years, and I do not miss it at all. In between my sessions and classes, I write, write, and write more.

My weekends are awesome. I dedicate one Saturday of the month to leading a group chanting and meditation session and another Saturday to giving workshops on different life-enhancing topics. My Sundays are mine to go to the beach, swim, walk, meditate with the sound of the ocean, and enjoy silence, sunshine, and a nice cup of café latté. Delicious lunch at a local café in Laguna or Newport Beach has always been my favorite.

I love what I do, and I am very grateful for the peace and contentment I feel in my heart. My life surely is my message.

Once a year, I take an exceptional trip just to review my life and reconnect to my purpose. This time, I took a month off of my full schedule in California and went to India—the motherland of yoga, meditation, reiki, devotional dances, sacred music, temples, mosques, churches, colors, spices, food, love, and much more. You name it, this place has it all.

I followed the signs on the road of my destiny to an absolute unknown and found myself in India, as you read in the first few pages. Since then, I have gone back at least once a year to cleanse and energize. I certainly had moments of being lost, but I soon found the light and pushed back on the road. Excited, tired, sad, happy, inspired, hopeless—I lived it all! I trusted the guides along the way and took one step at a time. I am here now.

The immense sense of belonging wraps its arms around me like a compassionate mother. I am home. Again, I sit in beautiful Kerala (Land of Gods), drinking hot delicious tea and reviewing my life to ignite the fire of inspiration in order to write and share my life story.

As I am sharing different stories with you, I realize how blessed I am to have had two masters/teachers in my life as my kids (Negin and Omid); to have been spoiled by the unconditional love of my little dog (Frosty) for fifteen years; and to have been touched by the angel of love in the form of friends and family all around the world. They honestly make the whole world my home.

I was able to continue my education to receive a PhD degree in Esoteric studies, which helped me to travel to mysterious places and lead unforgettable classes and conferences in many parts of the world. My profession as a reiki master/teacher, Yukt yoga/meditation professor, and past-life regression/future-life progression therapist is an honor and a privilege that allows me to serve thousands.

Just like you, I have faced all kinds of gigantic and tiny losses, challenges, and wins. For sure, I have not had a dull moment in my life, and not for a fraction of a second have I felt bored. Oh no, not me! I am a traveler on an exciting path, following the signs on a winding road. The happenings in my life are the unlimited source of inspiration for all that I did, do, and will do from this point on. They changed who I was, am, and will be—a monument I call "me," always under renovation, restoration, and repair. This is how life continues, as a stream of experiences, forever flowing and never ending, through life and beyond.

14

Write Kid

Life is a message: spread it.

Thursday November 29, 2018, 7:40 a.m.
Kerala, India
Somatheeram Ayurveda village

Slept well last night after my long twenty-four-hour journey to gorgeous Kerala from Los Angeles. The flight was easy and comfortable, though long. I honestly do not know why I chose to come to this place to stay for a month. I am not sure where the story goes, and I am not worried about it. All I know is I made a decision to stop everything in the United States and be here by myself. I was craving quiet time to be. No plans, no schedule, just "be with me" time.

This is my first time visiting Kerala. That familiar feeling of knowingness and ease is prevalent here as well. It feels as if I have been here many more times. I am not surprised at all. I chose Somatheeram Ayurveda village; needed some "spoil me" time with hot herbal oil massages garnished with simple, healthy, wholesome food, yoga, meditation, and a quiet space to write. I have it all here. It is exactly the way I imagined it to be.

Here, people are very simple, even more simple and friendly than people in the northern part of India. I guess it is the presence of the ocean and lush green lands that make Kerala so peaceful and special.

I lose track of time. I ask the hostess at the restaurant, where I sit daily for hours, to gather my thoughts and share my words:

"Excuse me, is it Thursday today?"

She smiles and says, "Let me check!" Mind you, she is not on vacation and did not have a twenty-four-hour flight. She comes back after few minutes with a beautiful smile on her face.

"Yes, ma'am, it is Thursday!"

Sweet. There is a deep sense of peace, even at work.

This is a great place for me to sit, sip warm comforting herbal tea, look at the ocean, listen to the birds, watch the trees and flowers, and write.

* * *

Come with me. Let us go back three years in time.

It is February 2015. I am in Brazil to witness the miracles of John of God. I sit with him every day for almost eight hours a day meditating with the entities of light to bring healing to the visitors of the casa. A few days ago, while meditating in the entities room where John of God receives thousands of people from all over the world for healing, I had a clear vision of Dr. Wayne Dyer instructing me to write. In that moment, with my eyes closed and my heart fully open to the universe, I simply asked, "How do I know this is you and not my imagination?"

Dr. Dyer's voice answered, "You will receive a pen before you leave this place. Accept it as a confirmation."

It is a precious piece of advice from my favorite author in spirit, Dr. Dyer, the father of spirituality at this time. It has been seven or eight years that I have been yearning to write a book about my experiences. But of course, excuse after excuse arises, and I procrastinate the project diligently.

I enjoy every day of my visit to the casa. I sit daily in meditation, holding space for John of God to help men, women, and children connecting to Saint Rita, the saint of impossibilities, to manifest miracles in their lives and transform the impossible into opportunity. Fourteen blessed days pass, and I face the last day of my visit. Time to leave the casa, taking the memory of magic and many miracles with me.

I am going to get on the shuttle to the airport. The trip is ending. I am so grateful for all that I observed and learned in these two weeks. It has been an absolutely incredible experience. I am going to hug Tom, my spirit godfather at the casa, to say goodbye when he picks up a pen from the table, hands it to me, and says, "Go back home and begin writing your memoir!" How did he know about me and writing? I never told him about it.

I burst into tears. I enter a trance like never before. The birth of this book is confirmed. I fly back home fired up to write.

* * *

And now I am in India, writing my unusual memoir. This is how life works.

Unfortunately, yesterday, I heard devastating news about John of God. I am not sure if you have been following the story of his human weakness and the collapse of his dedication to the path of healing. It created waves of pain and devastation for many in this world. For years, people came to seek healing through him, and the casa became the home of hope. By not honoring his prophecy, he shut the door of hope forever on thousands of men and women in search of health and healing.

If the news is accurate, I must say, he did not just rape women physically; he raped humanity. He raped the wounded, the helpless, and the hopeless. He committed the biggest crime of the century. He shot compassion in the heart, and he murdered trust.

Miracles happened at the casa. The simple and sweet story behind my writing is one of those, and I am forever thankful for the energy of the place and the guidance of the entities of light at the time of my visit. The clear vision of Dr. Dyer surely opened my consciousness to accept help from the heavens in order to express my feelings through the words dancing gracefully on these pages.

John of God is another soul in human form who did not understand the shower of blessings offered to him in this reincarnation. I am not shocked by the news. He is not the first one, and for sure won't be the last, who chose to embrace the monster of self-indulgence and greed. Once you step to the land of ego, the realm of darkness welcomes you with open arms.

Live like a lotus. Rise above the mud.

15

From What~
If to What Is

Life is a wave; ride it.

What if we change the annoying, doubtful, hesitant, and suspicious *if* in our lives to perfectly balanced, easy, and comforting *is*? Think about it. Instead of regretting, blaming, and being anxious in life, let us change our reality to what is and take responsibility for what we are experiencing right now. Being accountable for letdowns and accomplishments encourages us to look back but move forward.

Yes, as we discussed earlier, we build or demolish, create or destroy, lead or mislead the reality we choose to live in. We partner with the universe to co-produce this masterpiece called life. This is not some New Age pretty sentence. This is the reality of how powerful we are with all that we have in our possession. We add to the world or we deplete it of the creative energy needed for the well-being of all. We are co- producers of the universe at this very moment. We participate in all that is going on in the world with the energy we add to it or withdraw from it. In every second of every day we add to or deduct from the shared greatness in the world.

Think about it: every deed of yours is registered in the book of the universe. Peace or war in the world is the perfect picture of the collective awareness of us human beings. Being rooted in kindness, compassion, service, and love guides our world toward magnificence. War, cruelty, hate, and anger lead us to the arms of darkness. We decide where the world is now and where it is going. I always say the day all soldiers give up their guns and refuse to go to war, no leader can create war on our planet. So every single person is involved to the destruction or creation of our world.

We have a choice, and that is a privilege—a clear choice of what to add or take away. One selfish act ripples out and affects all life, in the same way one selfless deed creates powerful waves to touch many hearts near or far. The energy travels on the wings of consciousness. What we put out there, we receive back, and that is a fact.

16

Thank You, Doctor

Life is love: be it.

Love yourself, take time off, and spend a few days alone to experience the closeness of your guardian angel to your heart. Allow the silence to lead you on your uniquely designed path.

Let me tell you another one of my interesting stories. A few years ago—to be exact, in 2008—I developed a severe allergy. I constantly had a blocked nose, which was extremely tiring and exhausting.

This is where the journey began. Yes, it all started about ten years ago. Nose rinse after nose rinse, aromatherapy oils, different pillows, new shampoos, soaps, and conditioners—you name it, I tried it all. And nothing worked.

I tried all the different modalities, but there was no sign of improvement. I had one hour of relief and then again back to misery. I am sure people with allergies can well understand the suffering I was experiencing.

One morning, after a sleepless night, I asked myself, *How about seeing a surgeon?* I made an appointment with an ENT specialist to say goodbye to snoring, sneezing, runny nose, and sleepless nights.

"Your entire nose is covered with polyps," said the doctor. "How can you even breathe? Only surgery can give you relief."

And all I asked was, "When do you have an opening?"

She checked her schedule and said, "September 11!"

No wonder! I said okay immediately and signed up to say goodbye to an unhealthy nose and uncomfortable nights.

September 11 arrived, and the surgery was successful. I could breathe from the first moment after anesthesia, despite my doctor's prediction. She had warned me that for at least three days, it would be impossible for me to breathe through my nose, but my nose decided otherwise. I could breathe easily.

Everything was moving in a perfect direction. What a relief! After the surgery, my doctor prescribed penicillin pills, but despite that, my body continued fighting a high fever. After five days, she stopped the penicillin and started me on another ten days of antibiotic. Usually I prefer not to take medication, and my body is not used to chemicals. Being on prescription drugs for fifteen days completely messed up my digestive system and left me with horrible bleeding diarrhea.

When I contacted my doctor, all I heard was, "It is normal. It is a side effect of the medication you are on."

Really? Here we go again!

What should I do now? She prescribed another ten days of antibiotics to kill the monster bacteria that was growing and causing havoc in my intestines. I could not even imagine getting on another cycle of heavy-duty drug.

Something was happening—another story was being shaped. But of course, I could not read it.

I put myself on a very restricted diet of bananas, toast, yogurt, potatoes, and boiled rice for a month while introducing the new horrific antibiotic to my weak body. I lost eight pounds and had no appetite and no energy.

One early morning, around two o'clock, something made me get out of my bed, turn on the computer, go to the New Age guru Mr. Google, and type *Ayurveda centers in Kerala/India*. I had to take this body to the source. I was not going to lie in bed and melt away.

After few clicks, I found my way to the website of Somatheeram Ayurveda village, which had been recommended by a very close friend who is a practitioner in the field of Ayurveda herself. A bright light bulb went on in my brain and lit the path from my conscious mind to my heart and made me say yes to this divine intervention. I was on the plane in no time. My heart and my mind agreed, after a very short and friendly meeting, and they made me book my ticket without a doubt. The conversation went something like this:

Brain: *Is this what you want to do?*

Heart: *Yes. I feel great about it. I must do it.*

Brain: *When do you want to go?*

Heart: *After Thanksgiving. I want to spend Thanksgiving with my kids.*

Brain: *For how long?*

Heart: *How about a month?*

Brain: *A month? Are you crazy? Not working for a month?*

Heart: *Hey, calm down and listen. I must be well to be able to work, and I don't want to rush the healing process. Yes: I need a month off to work on myself!*

My heart won. It was the end of the year. Classes were not very busy, and this would be a great way to wrap up this year and open myself to new beginnings.

My heart continued gently, *You know what? Work on your 2019 resolutions. How about that? Or I better change it to 2019 revolution! Out with the old patterns and in with a new life.*

I had to bargain with my brain to accept my heart's sensible suggestion. And of course, my heart won the debate. I purchased my ticket, exchanged a few emails with the Ayurveda village, packed my bag, and was on my way to welcome a renewed, healthy body. Oh boy. I made the perfect decision.

* * *

Today is the second day in Ayurveda heaven, and I love it so much already.

Most people back home following the culture of suing each other were suggesting that I take legal action against the hospital and the doctor. But instead, I decided to go on a month long cleansing, purifying, and rejuvenating retreat. Which one would you choose?

I say happiness is a choice. Things happen along the way. We face difficulty, disease, discomfort, heartbreak, heartache, and so forth and so on. We can choose to look at each misfortune as a pathway to learning and an opportunity to change. I always find this path more effective, more interesting, and more attractive.

I gifted myself a month of tranquility with no schedule, no cooking, and no cleaning to focus on my new-year plan, to be present, to communicate clearly with the universe, to accept new ideas, and to let go of old patterns. I must stay grounded and faithful to my new wants and desires. I am clear about what I want. There is no time for doubt. I send the request to my higher consciousness with ultimate positivity and await manifestation. I know that the universe has my best interest at heart, and all will happen in divine order and according to divine timing, so no rushing it.

A spiritual journey happens on a single-lane road—one lane prepared only for one traveler, who is you. There is no wishing and praying to become something or someone. We are who we are in essence, waiting to be discovered by the self. Being whole by yourself is the key to spiritual evolution.

Just like everyone else on this planet, I have lived through heartbreaks, heartaches, joy and bliss. Time to pay attention to my weaknesses and my strengths. I have been vulnerable at times and have experienced the fullness of my feminine power or Shakti at other times. I have learned the value of each teardrop and the importance of each smile. Appreciating friends and family when I found myself lonely and unloved has always been a source of hope, reminding me of so much love and support that could last me many lifetimes. It is great to know that I am never alone.

I stumbled upon myself in the darkness of my thoughts and was touched by the brilliant light when least expected. I learned to trust and have faith in me, the angels, my guides on earth and in heaven, and most importantly, in God. I name this energy God, you can call it intelligence, awareness, super-consciousness, or anything else. Words don't matter. For me another name for it is *love*. The source of our existence. Naming it is not easy, feeling it is natural. It just is.

This form of energy has no beginning and no end, no religion, no color, cast, or creed. The energy has no form or shape. It is intangible, inaudible, and cannot be seen. It exists within and without. It is everywhere and nowhere. You cannot box it, label it, or store it. It is available to me, to you, and to all plants and animals.

It cannot be named. By naming it, you will shrink it. It does not care if you wear a hijab or walk naked. It does not belong to white people, black people, or people of another race. It does not live in temples, mosques, churches, or synagogues. This energy does not care if you grow your hair and wear a turban or shave your hair all the way to the skin. It does not see you as you appear. It sees and feels your vibration. This energy does not know you by your name, education, occupation, or bank account. It just sees your light.

The energy of love protects all. It navigates us through the winding roads of life. This is the energy of the pure intelligence, of light and awareness. It measures us by our compassion towards the self and all. In the eye of love, we are one, and there is no hierarchy. The energy of love does not care about our differences but celebrates our oneness. It is time to connect to it, live it, spread it, and be it.

The guidance comes from unexpected sources. This time, it was packaged in the form of tiny antibiotic capsules to push me to discover the rest of my life. I am grateful. Thank you, doctor!

Most sweet new beginnings are wrapped in bitter endings.

17

Forgiveness Heals

Life is magic: do not doubt it.

Yesterday was another beautiful and enlightening day at the Ayurveda village. I had my treatments in the morning, which includes detoxifying Abhyanga full-body massage, insightful shirodhara, and relaxing facial massage with a papaya face mask. I feel spoiled to the bone.

I met a few interesting people and had dinner with two ladies from Switzerland and another lovely lady from France, sharing our stories as old friends do. This is the main reason to take a few weeks off every year, traveling to different parts of the world by myself to meet others walking the path of spirituality in their own fascinating ways.

When you travel with friends and family, you stay in your comfort zone; but if you are by yourself, you expand and get a chance to touch other lives and be touched by other stories. Your heart smiles, your soul soars, and your mind gets totally entertained. For me stepping out of my world and following the signs to the unknown is the most inspiring and exciting part of traveling by myself.

There are many other stories and numerous worlds you can be part of with no conditioning. You spend a few days together and then part ways as if nothing happened. You might forget the names, but you will always remember the vibration and the energy you have received through these special interactions. They stay safe in your memory bank forever.

Now it is 7:15 a.m. I am sitting in the café enjoying my tasty hot cup of tea with a dash of honey while feeling the cool breeze on my face, hearing the roar of the ocean and the uplifting song of the birds. A rooster is singing in the distance, and crows are calling each other to say good morning. Butterflies are everywhere in multiple colors, and the smell of the freshly made Ayurvedic breakfast is intoxicating.

Yes, I am in heaven. This is pure *is*-ness, appreciating every moment and celebrating every single breath with no guarantee for the next. *Now* with capital *N*. This is what I have in this very moment, with no promise of tomorrow.

I have another great story to share with you. Grab a cup of your favorite tea or coffee, relax, and listen to my story.

* * *

It is May 2017, a few days before my birthday, when I see an advertisement on Facebook about a magic show by David Minkin, an amazing award-winner for close-up magic. I immediately call Omid, my son, and ask him if he wants to accompany me to see the show.

Omid is a standup comedian. He travels the world and brings laughter to the lives of many. By the way, when he started comedy at the age of nineteen, I was a great subject for his material! I loved it. He is funny. He knows many entertainers of different genres. He is quite surprised by my request.

"Mom, a magic show? Since when you are interested in magic shows?"

"I don't know. Just something about this ad and David. I must go to see him."

"Okay, let me see. I will get the tickets," Omid says. "I know David, and yes, he is awesome."

"Thank you. Make sure you do it."

"Okay, Mom."

* * *

Days pass with no news from Omid. The craving for this magic show grows even deeper in my heart. There is something about it I cannot express with words.

A few weeks later, I ask, "Omid, did you get the tickets?"

"Oh no, Mom, I forgot."

"Just tell me if Friday, August 11, works for you," I say, "and I will get the tickets now."

"Sure, Mom, do it. Go ahead."

I went online and started the process of purchasing two tickets when I felt the urge to invite my daughter. Negin is a busy young woman, living in Los Angeles with her lovely husband, Robin, and two naughty dogs: Mr. Moon, a black Chihuahua, and Miss Rani, a white one. Negin is the executive director of the Santa Monica Pier and has a full schedule. She loves art and entertainment. Oh boy, she is great at creating art and bringing gifted artists of all different talents together. With her busy life, I doubt she will accept the invitation but let's call her anyway.

This is what I am expecting to hear from her: *Friday evening magic show? Why? No thank you, Mom. I am busy.*

Surprisingly, she says, "Yes, sure. Robin will be out of town. I am available and would love to join you guys. But Mom, a magic show? For real?"

Yes yes yes. I want to go to this show.

Now I am really excited. Getting both of them to agree to accompany me to the show is magic by itself. I pick up my credit card to buy three tickets when I feel this strange feeling to call their dad, my ex-husband, and invite him to the show as well, not knowing why.

After our divorce, we were not very close. The four of us haven't been out together for ages. But some strong and very strange, unknown, but pleasantly loving force compels me to make the phone call.

"Hi, Banka."

"Hi," he says. "How are you?"

"I am doing great," I answer.

"I am taking the kids to a magic show by David Minkin on Friday," I tell him. "Would you like to join us?"

"A magic show? Wow. Now you are interested in magic shows?"

"Yes. I want to go to this show, though I don't know why. Are you available?"

"Sure," he answers. "I have two business guests meeting me here from Hong Kong, and I am going to take them to Vegas on Saturday, but I can join you all on Friday. Thank you for inviting me," he adds.

"Awesome," I reply.

"Do you want to ride with me?" he asks. "Come and park your car in my garage, and we will go together. I know how much you don't care for driving.

"Sure, thank you."

"How about having dinner before the show?" he asks.

"I will ask Negin to find a nice restaurant close to the venue and reserve a table for four," I suggest.

"Great. See you at six thirty on Friday."

I hang up the phone, not knowing the real magic is on the way.

* * *

My daughter makes a reservation for us at a cozy little Greek restaurant to eat before the show.

On the way to the restaurant, my son calls to see where we are. We have a pleasant conversation, laughing about my sudden interest in magic shows.

My son pauses for a moment and says, "The two of you in one car? How strange!"

We all laugh. It is nice to be together, the four of us eating, laughing, and having simple fun. The show is incredible. I am totally mesmerized by David. He is awesome.

It is time to say goodbye. I am going to spend the night at my daughter's home. So in the parking lot, we say goodbye to each other. Omid is flying to London the next day, and his dad is going to India on Monday to attend an engagement party and is quite excited about it.

We had a great evening. On our way to Negin's home, she even mentions how happy Dad was that night.

* * *

A few days pass. Omid is in London performing in comedy clubs, and his dad is in India enjoying the preparation for the engagement party. On

August 25, the four of us are on a group text talking to each other. It is half an hour before my meditation class— powerful class on the Tao Te Ching.

After exchanging few texts, I sign off to attend my class. Right before starting the class, a weird, unfamiliar feeling makes me check my phone one last time. I see many phone calls and texts from Omid. How strange!

"Mom, Negin, call me," he has texted few times, and he has left numerous voicemails.

I call and ask, "What happened? Why are you calling? Is everything okay?"

"Mom, Dad died." A short and cold sentence with no meaning at all.

"Whose dad?"

"Our dad. My dad just had a massive heart attack and died."

"Who told you?"

"My cousin."

Time stops. He is no more! It hurts. I cannot talk, I cannot think. I pause, a long pause. It really hurts.

"What should I do now, Mom?" he asks.

In less than a few minutes, our lives have changed.

"Fly to India immediately," I tell him. "Get there as soon as you can."

The world stops, but the clock keeps on moving. Tick-tack, tick-tack, and the dance of life continues to the music of time without a pause.

I walk in total disbelief to my meditation class. I sit there numb, feeling his presence around me. I hear his voice: *You will love it here. It is all that you teach.* He has disappeared, leaving me wondering about the magic of life.

Suddenly, everything makes sense: my unwavering wish to go to the show together, the timing, the venue, the subject, all orchestrated in a way that no human mind could plan and implement. It was his last scene—the last time my kids ate, laughed, and had fun with their dad. That night was his last appearance in the magic show of life.

A few days later, I call David Minkin and talk to him for about two hours, sharing with him the close-up magic he brought to the life of my family. He is grateful to know that he was part of such a real-life magic show.

This existence is nothing but pure magic. The show must go on, and this was Banka's magical curtain call.

18

I Believe in Angels: Day 4 in Heaven

Life is short; enjoy it.

Yesterday ended so beautifully. Life is amazing when you open up to the gifts being offered to you. I had a wonderful, fun-filled, and most insightful dinner with my new friends from Switzerland and France. We exchanged life stories. Some were quite mind-boggling.

Every day passed is permission to move ahead. We learn from the past but move forward. Each day's lessons are gifts wrapped in colorful emotions. Open the gift, toss the wrapper, but keep the teachings. Allow life to unfold; let go of the trash and treasure the present.

This very moment is another gift. Be excited to open it, learn from it, thank it, and at the end of the day, let it all go. Every night before falling asleep, give all that the universe offers you back to the source with ultimate

98

gratitude. Empty yourself and your heart, and be available for all the mystery and magic of tomorrow.

Life is a beautiful intricate mandala. Be present to adorn it with your colorful learnings. At the sacred time of transition from this form, nothing gets lost. We never finish; we continue in another form. Our life is a continuance from one vibration to the next, from form to formless, matter to energy and back. We move on and on to reach the state of "Moksh" or enlightenment. Moksh or spiritual enlightenment is the end of our returning to the body and is the state of pure consciousness.

We came from "no-where to Now-here heading back to no-where." For some of us who believe in the process of reincarnation, death is a much easier concept to understand, accept, and process. It helps us not to see death as a full stop but an extension.

When a soul departs, we miss the touch, the smell, the sight, and the sound of our loved one. After a healthy process of grief, we begin feeling them anytime, all the time, anywhere, and everywhere. We make an incredible connection to the intangible sense of presence. We do not see them, but we feel them. We can find them in another frequency easily and effortlessly only if we rid ourselves of sadness and prolonged sorrow.

On this topic, I have another amazing story to share with you—a truly life-changing experience. Time for another cup of steaming tea, I guess. Sit back, relax, and follow me into the pages.

* * *

It is 2005, and I am teaching at the American Board of Hypnotherapy— the amazing ABH conference. Speakers and students gather from all over the world to share and learn about the hypnotic state, watch fun stage hypnosis, get in touch with their own psychic abilities, and have fun bending spoons and forks with the power of their mind. Past-life regression sessions and remote-viewing classes are among the many interesting topics.

Every year, I teach Reiki, reflexology and meditation at the conference, initiating many to the healing concept of Reiki. We are also here to build extraordinary friendships to last a lifetime or just for this one week. Both are valuable in their own unique nature. The energy is fabulous.

As speakers at the event, we have the privilege of attending other speakers' sessions in our free time. So let me tell you a story about one of these incredible classes. Let us go back in time to one of the days at the conference. An unbelievable story.

I feel very excited today. I know that something amazing is going to happen, either in one of my own classes or in another class that I will be taking. I look at the brochure to pick a class that fits my schedule. Here we go: Shelly, a brilliant hypnotherapist, is offering a meditation session guiding participants to connect with their guardian angels. I love it. I am a believer. I feel the energy of my angels always and in all different ways.

So let's do it.

I reach the class fifteen minutes early to unwind and relax. I always choose the first row for focus and less disturbance. This is a super-special topic. Shelly is a gifted teacher and connected to the realm of the nonphysical. She is an expert in her craft, and I am ready to explore.

The door opens, and a lady who does not look very happy walks in. She looks lost and sad. She sits next to me. My eyes catch her name badge: oh my God, "Vicki"! I lost my best friend Vicki a few weeks prior to the conference. She made her transition after battling a horrifying cancer. She moved on and left many of us witnessing the impermanence of life once more. A young, energetic, successful, beautiful woman just vanished. I miss my friend a lot—and this is a sign that she is here.

I breathe, and all of a sudden, I feel this immense connection with the Vicki sitting next to me. I want to say hello, but she tries so hard to ignore me. There is no eye contact, and her body language screams, "Leave me alone."

"Hi. Good morning," I say anyway.

Just to be polite, she mumbles, "Hi." She is obviously not in the mood to socialize or even to be in the session

"How is your day?" I ask

"I hate every minute of it," she grumbles. "A friend of mine forcefully brought me here to this nonsense. I just want to leave."

"Oh, I am sorry to hear that. Shelly is great, and her class about the angels is an extraordinary experience."

"I don't believe in any of this. I want to go home. I don't need to be connected to any angel. I don't have an angel. I want to go home now!" she almost screams.

Shelly walks in at this point. Her energy is bubbly and fun—very light and easy. She laughs all the time and makes people laugh often during her class. She is one of my favorites for sure.

"How is everyone?" she asks.

"Great!" most of us reply.

But Vicki is annoyed. She is fidgety. She moves so much. She is very irritated and uncomfortable. Yet she does not leave the class. I am glad that she is with us. I hope she receives a comforting message from her angel. I keep her in my prayers for an extraordinary experience.

And the meditation is about to begin.

"Sit comfortably," Shelly begins. "Take a few nice deep breaths."

Shelly continues after a relaxing meditation, "Focus on the area around your ears. Clear the energy there to be able to hear the voice of your angel. Focus on the area in between your eyes. Clear your third eye to see the form of your angel. Focus on your heart to be able to feel the loving presence of your angel in your heart. Be still, stay focused, be open, and do not doubt."

Finally, she asks, "Can you see your angel?"

Yes. My angel comes in the majestic form of a magnificent eagle soaring in the sky above. I am mesmerized by such beauty and grace. I watch in complete silence and awe.

"What is the name of your angel?" asks Shelly.

My angel's name is Bob.

Here we go again, Kathy. Bob? Bob is the name of your angel? Dive deeper. It must be Michael, Raphael. Are you sure? Bob? This is my mind talking, by the way.

Shelly says, "Don't doubt."

And I center myself, taking deep breaths, letting go of the chatter in my mind.

"What is the message from your angel?" Shelly asks.

I am hearing a very clear message from Bob the angel. He says, "I love you. I never left you. I am always with you. Please be happy for me. I am happy, I am fine, and I am where I want to be."

Bravo Kathy! What imagination! Bob your eagle angel wants you to know that he is okay and happy? What a waste of a session! My disappointed mind mutters.

Shelly guides us to take deep breaths, stretch our body, and gently open our eyes.

The meditation took about forty-five minutes. I am so disappointed. I missed the chance of getting connected with my angel. I think to myself, *Bob? Who is Bob?*

Most people are thrilled with their experience, but I am totally confused. *Who is Bob?* I wonder again.

After a few minutes of silence, Shelly asks if anyone wants to share.

Hands go up. I am silent and kind of embarrassed at the same time. I'll just keep quiet and try not to make eye contact with Shelly. *You will be fine*, my mind suggests. Hopefully Shelly will not pick you to share your experience with the class.

We listen to a few amazing, enchanting stories about angels and archangels. People are emotional, crying, smiling, and in my head, I am questioning Bob.

"Kathy," Shelly calls out, "you always have great stories. Would you like to share?"

O Lord! Please save me.

"Mine might be the funniest of all angel stories, Shelly."

I look at Vicki, thinking to myself that my story might bring a smile to her face. After all, I had a funny vision.

I take a deep breath and start. "My angel came in the form of an eagle. A huge, mighty eagle."

I can hear Vicki's labored breath at this point. She turns toward me, looking at me for the first time. *Hope she is okay*, I think to myself, and I continue my story.

"His name was Bob."

Oh my God, Vicki is crying so hard. Everyone is looking at her. She is shaking uncontrollably. I hold her in my arms

She is trying to say something, but she cannot. We all are patiently awaiting peace to overcome her sadness.

Finally, in broken words, she says, "Bob … Bob is my twin brother who was in love with eagles. He moved from California to Colorado to be able to go eagle-watching daily. He bought a home on top of a hill, drove daily on a winding road to work. A week ago, he met with an accident and died at the scene. My friend insisted that I must come to this conference to get closure through meditations, hypnosis, and other experiences. I hated every minute of it till now …"

I am amazed and totally speechless but in gratitude with all there is. I am thankful for the strong connection with my friend Vicki to create a pathway between the three of us. Vicki and I got connected in this room through love. We invited the angry Vicki to join the reunion for healing. Three souls on earth and in spirit, one and inseparable. Do you believe in the oneness of all?

This is my learning from the experience. The girl is filled with grief, anger, and sadness. I am open and bursting with love for my friend Vicki. Bob wants to give a message to his sister, but she is not available. I am sitting next to her completely open and totally accessible. Bob chooses me to convey the message to his sister.

Job well done, Bob!

Thank you, Bob. Thank you, Vicki. I am forever grateful to you both and to Shelly for facilitating this connection.

Class is over and it is time to go to lunch with my new friend Vicki and to send her off with so much love from her caring brother Bob, the eagle angel in spirit. She left with a heart full of love and gratitude.

I am so blessed to be in the right place at the right time once more. Thank you, universe, for leading me where you need me.

19

Frosty Boy

Life is your guru; follow it.

Time for my favorite story and maybe another cup of steamy hot herbal tea for you. Relax and feel this heartwarming experience. This slice of my life is very precious to me and feels way bigger than life. It refined my soul and made me a better human being.

This is the story about my most valuable teacher: my soul-baby. He taught me kindheartedness, unreserved love, patience, the importance of surrender, and trust. This great master transformed my reality and reformed my life in every possible way. He planted the seed of respect toward all life on the planet in my heart to carry me through this physical reincarnation and after.

* * *

Let me take you back in time to April 2001. My son, Omid, is turning twelve in a week. He is in love with something that I can never figure out: video games.

"Omid, what do you want for your birthday this year?" I ask.

"Can I have an Xbox, Mom? Please, can I have one?"

"Sure, we will go to the mall on Sunday to pick one up for you."

We plan and God laughs. When we arrive at the mall, it is six in the evening, and the stores are closing.

"I am sorry, Omid. We will come another day to get your Xbox."

He is quite disappointed.

To cheer him up, I suggest, "How about a nice ice cream at Fashion Island?"

"Okay, let's go!"

Omid, Negin and I are having a great day. Fashion Island is an open-air mall, a fun place to spend the evening. We are walking around aimlessly. Nothing to do, just having a lazy, pleasant Sunday evening.

"Can we go to the pet shop, Mom?" Both kids started jumping around, begging me.

"Guys, you know how scared I am of dogs," I say, trembling. "You know well that I cannot be close to any dog. Even the thought of being close to a dog makes me quite uncomfortable." It is embarrassing but true.

"Mom, please? They are in cages. Nothing will happen. Please?" And of course, they drag me into the pet shop.

The moment we walk in, my body begins shaking uncontrollably from head to toe. The smell of the pet shop takes me back to that cold, snowy winter evening getting off the bus and walking home from piano lesson in Tehran. I am only fifteen years old.

The street is covered in fluffy snow. Icicles are hanging off tree branches. No one is on the street. The silence is alarming. It is getting dark. I better hurry home. I can hear my feet kissing the snow in every step. I begin walking a bit faster when I feel the presence of a few homeless dogs behind me. I am scared. My heart is beating fast. I start to cry and begin to run.

They are barking loud and running behind me. I let go of my books, notes, and purse. I fall a few times, and my pants rip. Blood is gushing from my knee. I am so scared.

A door is open. I run inside, shut the door, and lose consciousness. A few hours later, I wake up in a stranger's home in shock and panic, not believing what has happened to me. My world has changed forever.

That day was the end of my connection to cats and dogs. For years, I feared dogs in all sizes, shapes, and forms. The smell of dogs churns my stomach.

"Let us get out of here, please," I almost cry.

"Mom, wait! Look at this little dog," Omid says.

A little white toy is knocking on the glass with his little paws as if to say, "Pick me! Pick me! Take me home!"

"Can I play with him?" Omid begs.

"No, let's go."

"Please, Mom?"

"Okay. Just for a few minutes."

I stand at the door of the pet shop away from this little guy, waiting to go home as soon as we can.

"Can we please take him home?" they both ask, and of course my answer is no.

That night, we go home with heavy hearts. The kids wanted the dog, but I was not ready to bring a dog home.

* * *

"Listen to me, please. It is impossible for me to live with a dog. Why don't you understand?"

"Mom, he is so little! He is not a wild dog, and he will not hurt you."

"I know, but I am still scared to death of any dog."

For days we have this discussion at home, and guess what? By the weekend, the kids win the battle. This little playful fur ball found his way into my kids' hearts and came home with us. My son named him Donut, but the dog was not responding to the name.

"Omid, how about Frosty?" I suggest. "He looks like a snowman with his black shiny eyes and charcoal black leathery nose."

I think to myself, *Oh God, he is too cute … as long as he stays away from me.*

We all agree on the name, and he seems to like it.

I am still scared of this one-pound sweet toy. I cannot touch him. I am not able to hold him or even sit close to him. What is wrong with me? All day, I pretend that I am okay, but seriously, I am not. A dog even this small makes me nervous.

* * *

Days pass, and we have to take Mr. Frosty to the vet for a checkup. My son is holding him, but Frosty is very nervous. He is shaking. I feel bad not being able to calm him down.

"You can hold him," the doctor says to me.

"Who, me?" I am panicked and embarrassed at the same time. My heart is racing. I have sweaty palms, and I feel that I am going to throw up right in that very moment.

"Yes, you. Hold him. You are the mom, aren't you?"

I mumble with hesitation, "Yes, I am."

"So hold him. He feels safe in your arms. He is a little baby."

I stretch my arms forward in full hesitancy, and he puts Mr. Frosty on my palms.

Oh my God, what is this I am holding? I close my eyes, bring him close to my heart, and hold my baby for the first time, feeling his heartbeat on the palms of my hands while his eyes look right into my soul as if my shivering body did not exist. He looks through me, and I lose my heart in an instant. For the first time, his presence fills my heart with utmost gratefulness. I lose my fear and reluctance in that moment and find love and appreciation in return. An instant connection forms that carries me through life for fifteen years. I am holding bliss in my arms.

I call it "love at first touch." I am in love with Mr. Frosty! He crawls into my heart and finds his way into my soul. We make a promise to be together in body and beyond.

* * *

For fifteen years, Frosty sat in all of my workshops, yoga and meditation sessions, and reiki training classes. He was present at all of our group chanting and celebrations. He was and still is a unique yogi.

My Frosty boy left his little body on November 15, 2016, and built a nest of light permanently in my heart. His sweet energy is still powerfully present in my everyday life.

The day he passed, I heard him in my meditation. He said, *I will connect to you through number seventeen.* Seventeen was an insignificant number for me, but I trusted the vision. That day I went with Sara, my spirit-daughter, to lunch. We were both crying and in deep grief. The bill came to seventeen dollars and seventeen cents! Yes, he made a promise to be around, and he sure kept it.

My wish is to see him once I cross over. Who knows?

* * *

Frosty became my buddy, my baby, my love, my friend, my everything. The bond and the love we shared had no match. It was love beyond form and shape. We connected through the tangible and intangible while in body and beyond.

The last day of his life, when he was preparing to cross over to be with the angels, was the hardest, most devastating day of my life. A few of us gathered in the hospital chanting the universal *Om* mantra to send his soul home. He passed at ease. I wanted him to be comfortable at the most sacred moment of his existence. He was going home.

I asked him to run to the angels once on the other side and do not worry about me. I told him: "My boy, I cannot hold your leash anymore. You are free. Go and be with your angel. I will be fine here. I will connect with you in your new form." He gave me a kiss and left his body easily and effortlessly.

He taught me how wonderful it is to surrender and trust. He was and still is my favorite teacher. With him, I entered the kingdom of animals once more, and he was there to teach me about the magnificence of connecting to our four-legged friends. He patiently helped me to reprogram my mind and to let go of suffocating fear. I learned to leave the past behind and embrace the future with his help.

He was present in the darkest moments of my life, and he was there to celebrate all the glory of the light. Frosty knew it all. He walked next to me through the ups and downs of life wagging his tail, saying, *This shall pass. I am with you.* The fear of dogs left me the moment I held him in my arms. He trained me to love and respect animals.

After transition to spirit, he moved from my home to my heart and retired comfortably there. *Frosty, I miss your touch, your barking, your smell, and most of all, I miss you ordering me around! Will see you on the other side, my little angel!*

I had to change my world to allow love in. I had to move from the state of fear and paranoia to the comforting state of trust and surrender. I could have easily let the love out, but I chose to give it a chance and open up to the change.

Change is bliss. It is the only permanent fact of life. Embrace it.

Thank you, Frosty boy, my little gigantic teacher in form and beyond.

20

Back to the Now ... Still in India

Life is magnificent: live it.

I am at one with the sun and the sand, inseparable from the birds, butterflies, trees, flowers, and ocean. Somatheeram Ayurveda village has been a generous host for the past five days. Kind and professional staff, out-of-this-world Ayurveda treatments, simple healthy food—it all comes together to create an experience of peace, tranquility, safety, and solace. It is a piece of heaven on earth.

I get out of my comfy bed at four o'clock in the morning. I make a cup of hot water; talk to Sara to make sure everything is in order at our home-temple in Irvine, California; take a quick shower; and begin my day by practicing two hours of yoga, reiki, and meditation on the beach.

My focus on this trip is to share my story to inspire men and women all around the world to honor their incredible power within. I want to invite you to see every event as an opportunity for living your purpose and bringing your message to life. You are a living, breathing message in a form. You are the divine intelligence, the Buddha dancing to the music of life. Your very own existence is your partner in this dance. Have fun with it, step in bliss, and pause in ecstasy.

Don't wait for others to guide you. Connect to the guru within. Let go of fear and doubt, trust your inner Buddha, and begin moving. Know that in tango, you are never alone. The divine is guiding you on your path.

You must surrender, stay close to the source, and follow the guidance that streams from within. Close your eyes, pause, listen, feel, trust, and follow.

I am holding the mirror so you can see your authentic self from within. You are beautiful, and your dance is powerful. Each new step destroys the last one and creates the next. So in each step, you create, preserve, and destroy. You embody Brahma (the creative energy), Vishnu (the protector), and Shiva (the destroyer) in one simple step. Your existence is not a casual happening. It is a grand appearance. Hold your head up, stand tall, and make it happen.

Invite love, the most powerful energy in the universe, to dance with you. Love heals. It sure keeps you young and attractive—not only the outside but the deepest part of your being shines bright once touched by the energy of love from within. When in love, dreams become colorful, and daydreaming is most wonderful.

Keep on dancing, my friend!

21

Meet Jean

Life is a game of chess; win it.

Back to the sacred now. I am still in Somatheeram, enjoying Ayurveda treatments for rejuvenation.

I love you, universe. Yesterday, I was introduced to an extremely powerful soul connection. Life is so kind to me. I met Jean! He lives in France. He speaks English with a very sweet accent. He feels real and authentic. I said hello to him in the morning at breakfast. I like his energy. He is a strong presence wrapped in a very gentle approach.

We sit together at lunch. We laugh for hours about our treatments. We look very funny: muddy, smelly, oily, and sweaty, with a thick mask of some kind on our faces, walking around in our ugly, loose, unfitted but comfy green robes after the treatment is done. Wearing this robe is your reminder to leave the world of superficiality behind and be yourself. Nothing to hide, nothing to be other than who you really are.

The moment you undress and wear this unfitted robe, the journey of self-discovery and self-love begins. You start your voyage to meet yourself. How comfortable you are with the person in the robe decides that day's journey. This is totally another reality where you do not care for your hair, makeup, jewelry, outfit, occupation, or title. You are in this reality to face yourself and to introduce yourself from within. It is you and only you present in this moment. There is no help from outside. You represent you—naked, real, and with nothing to cover you. Stripped of all illusions, you are bare, raw, alone, and exposed.

Here, most of us seem to be relaxed about it. We walk around with no care in the world, living our stories and creating new paintings of our lives—a new friend, a fresh love, an original story all together.

$$* * *$$

It is a fun lunch. Jean, Sakshi, Oksana and Mimi—my new friends from different parts of the world—and I sit together, eat, and laugh out loud about what goes on in our treatment rooms. We are having fun. We act like teenagers, the childlike innocence coloring our days in such bright and amusing hugs. I want to live in this reality endlessly—beautiful moments captured in our hearts forever. It does not matter where this road is taking us. All I can feel is: Yes! This is real!

As Jean mentions at dinner, one hour of this life is way more precious than ten years of a disabled and broken togetherness. Being in a labored relationship that needs so much effort and doing is exhausting. This is a less-doing and more-being connection, and we love it. Every moment is refreshing, effortless, and most precious.

We decide to meet for dinner at seven thirty and go to Manaltheeram, the sister property that is walking distance from ours. But of course, this is India, and you can always ask for a taxi. We get into our white, clean, air-conditioned taxi with beautiful white seat covers and a courteous driver. We are on our way to make more unforgettable memories.

The taxi ride takes just a few minutes. The air is warm and comforting. It is dark, and the inviting light of the candles is our guide. It is easy to feel the gentleness of the cool breeze on your skin as a kind hostess.

Welcome to the sanctuary. The ocean makes sure that we hear her voice. She is singing the song of friendship and bond. Her song is a reminder of the impermanence of all, even the bond we are making today in this very moment. She reminds us of the waves of energy in our lives. She warns us of the briefness of this moment. Every time a wave kisses the shore, it washes all of the old memories that were made even a few moments ago and moves them back to the source. So she reminds us to be intimate with this very moment, to take it all in, and not to waste a precious second. Find each other, recognize the connections, feel the vibrations, follow, one step forward, one step back, and allow the dance to go on.

There are five of us at dinner: me; Mimi, our French doll; Sakshi, our spicy twenty-three-year-old Indian princess; Jean, the gentle-man from France; and lady Oksana from Ukraine. Oksana is so sweet. We communicate through signs and internet, since her English is not that fluent. We understand her clearly, and she understands us very well with not many words. We communicate through our hearts, loud and clear, and we get lost in our amazing conversations with a very limited vocabulary.

We create a fascinating, one-world global group, spending a lot of time together exchanging stories to cry or laugh about. The universe brought us here to help and to heal each other. We all know it, and we appreciate and honor this togetherness.

The *is*-ness of this moment is incredible. It allows us to be our true, authentic selves with no judgment. There is no room for the past or the future. The now is the only place we want to be. In a few days, we all will be in our homes somewhere in the world, carrying memorable and dazzling memories of each other, something to giggle about when life gets tough. Knowing that somewhere in the world there is a heart who knows mine is a comforting, irreplaceable sensation. We are blessed to find each other.

* * *

The topic we are led to talk about at dinner is love. Of course, it is always about love. I am certainly here to release all of the past heartaches and give love another chance. There is no other way to live but to let go, pause, reflect, understand, open my heart wholly, and trust in the wisdom of the universe.

Once I heard, "The one you are seeking is seeking you." I choose to make this meaningful sentence my reality.

I raise my vibration and send clear signals to the universe announcing my presence: *I am here, hello. Look at me, read me, understand me, and allow me to manifest the good, the great, and the magnificent in my life.*

I am ready to connect. This is not the time to doubt or question. It is the perfect time to embrace the energy with every level of my consciousness. Allowing liveliness to fill up my entire existence feels great.

Being ready is not enough either. I must be willing to follow, as Jean reminds me with so much tenderness and compassion. Every so often we want to lead, but reading the code and following the guidance can push many rusted doors open.

Jean is a tango lover. "In tango, we must be willing to follow each other's energy," he says. "If we both lead, we will fall. Each one of us must find our rhythm and center the self."

But isn't this true about life as well? Now the title of my book makes sense, right? *The Buddha's Tango* is the dance of consciousness.

* * *

I thought about Jean's comments last night before falling asleep and today during yoga. I always wanted to lead. I am a leader. I can do it. I can do it for me, I can do it for you, I can do it for everyone. This is the script I played most of my adult life.

Jean is my earth-angel. We met for a special reason, which will unfold on its own divine timing.

Are you ready for another unbelievable story? Relax and take it all in. This is a fun story regarding the power of belief.

* * *

"Jean, what is your full name?" I ask.

"Jean Xavier Roehri."

"Oh, I can hear the sound of *Ray* in his name," I say to myself. "Do you play chess?"

"How do you know?" He looks quite shocked by my question.

"Well, do you?"

"Yes. I started playing chess at age six. It changed my life. Why do you ask these questions? How do you know, Kathy?"

"I don't know," I tell him. "I am just asking."

I have to pause, take a breath, and tell him my crazy experience, hoping he understands.

The night before my trip to India, I was in meditation seeking the answer for my trip to Kerala and staying in Somatheeram for a whole month. My excuse was detoxing my body off of the antibiotics I had taken after my nasal polyp surgery, but I was not convinced.

I am sure you have those moments when you feel someone is sitting next to you talking, but in reality, there is no one around. Sometimes the voice is so real it gives you no choice but to listen. The same thing happened to me that night in meditation. I had a voice that I could hear, and it was so clear and reassuring that I had to follow.

This is what I heard: "You will meet a man in India who has the sound of *Ray* in his name. And your clue to recognize him is: he plays chess."

"But why do we meet? What is next?" I asked the mystery voice. "Please, someone, anyone? What is the reason for this union?" I asked, but no answer.

"Come on, tell me!" I insisted.

"Follow the signs," I heard. "It is for you both to discover. We just bring you together. You must choose the next step. You are the creator of the next chapter."

And the voice died out.

"Which signs do we have to follow?" I asked. But there was no clear answer.

I had the most relaxing sleep that night. Something was shifting. I did not know what, but it was quite exciting.

* * *

Jean looks astonished when I tell him about my vision.

"Okay," he says, "let us follow the signs, Kathy. There is no other option but to follow."

During our sweet and fun conversation at dinner, Jean reminds me of the importance of following in tango. It hits home. It really does.

I understand. I must step aside, surrender, not ask irrelevant questions, and just allow the energy to guide me and to take me where I need to be. I must trust the guidance that comes fully and freely from the Buddha within and follow the steps in the tango of life.

This is not a time to doubt. I must be available and ready to dance. I want to dance to the end of life.

* * *

Jean is going to give me a tango lesson today after lunch. I cannot wait. We definitely chose to meet not knowing why. Maybe he is here to lead me, and I am here to practice the art of following. We chose to share this time together. We are present to hold each other's hands, to synchronize our steps, and to follow the tune with no resistance. I feel that we are both ready.

It is time to celebrate our effortless and unplanned togetherness. We must trust that if one of us falls, the other will be there to catch. We will not lose each other; we are in this together. The key is to relax and allow the consciousness to take us, and for sure it is okay not to know what is next.

Jean has been dancing tango for eight or nine years. He is really good at it. But this time, it is quite different. He is dancing to the music of life. Our stage is our lives. We must center ourselves and take conscious steps recognizing each other's presence in this very moment and in this special place: Somatheeram/Kerala.

In tango, the man feels the energy in his heart. The posture is to keep the chest forward and the heart open to the powerful exchange of energy. This is how he leads the way. The woman's role is to read the energy and respond to the vibration she receives. If the man comes forward, the woman must step back, and if he steps back, she must come forward. This is how life is. Feel, understand, trust, allow, pause, and follow the gentle lead of energy to take the next step. This is the Buddha's tango.

I am so very grateful for today and my first ever tango lesson. Wow, what a wonderful feeling. I remember last year, I watched *Shall We Dance?* a few times. It was quite inspiring. I am going to sign up for dance lessons when I return home, and once I get fluent in the language of tango, I will meet Jean somewhere in this world to dance with him. At the present moment, I do not know where and when, but I am sure our strong connection will plan it, and we will have no choice but to follow.

I feel so special and blessed for the kindness and gentleness of the universe at this time of my life. Life is tremendously kind to me. I am at the stage of my life where what I need is peace, kindness, and tenderness, and I have it all at this point. Life has been generous to me.

* * *

After our tango lesson, Jean suggests we walk on the beach together. "Great, sure, let's go," I agree.

It is another unforced but powerful experience. The sun is about to set. It is taking its time. The sun is not in a hurry in any way but welcomes the clouds to pass it by. The sun is patient and easygoing.

We find two beach beds next to each other. It is the perfect picture of how life is supposed to be. I call it simple abundance. The goddess painted this moment with such delicacy and care. She does not want anything to stain this pearly white canvas.

There is no hurry, no rush. This is another example of heavenly timing, all in divine order. The sun is smiling, birds are flying, the ocean is singing, clouds are dancing, and the earth is patiently and quietly witnessing all this beauty.

Jean lies down.

I ask permission to touch him. We are preparing for Reiki. I call upon Jean's angels and mine to accompany and help us in the healing process of Reiki. This is an exchange for my tango lesson—a unique expression of our special friendship.

He seems to be comfortable and at ease. Everything sounds and looks flawless, and if there exists an imperfection, we find balance and perfection in the midst of it all.

I close my eyes and begin connecting.

"Jean, do you know Albert?"

"Yes. He is my father."

"Do you know Patricia?"

"Yes. My sister."

"Do you know Elizabeth/Lisa?"

"Yes. My sister's daughter is Lisa." Later he tells me that she was named after his grandmother, Elizabeth.

Okay, the connection is strong and clear. We are now connected through the web of Reiki. Our energies recognize each other, and we have permission to enter each other's unlimited, unending, infinite field of consciousness.

The dance of energy begins. One step forward, one step back. One breath in, one breath out. Completely synchronized, measured, planned, and at the same time, free of rules and regulations, stepping into the unknown, the realm of all possibilities. The body stays still, witnessing the tango of souls. There is a magnificent, brilliant, ongoing flow to follow.

Through the guidance of Reiki, I get to the root cause of any discomfort. I read the information in the person's aura and change the codes in the field of energy for healing to occur. I am just a channel. I do not heal but make it possible for the soul to find its way and the body to open up to the process of healing. I call myself an active observer in the process of Reiki. Keeping the music alive while monitoring the intimacy of soul, emotions, and body—a simple but at the same time sophisticated process—is what I do.

Being an active witness keeps the vibration up, the path clear of obstacles, and the light bright to create oneness of body, mind, and spirit. This is my job while in Reiki.

I look for Jean and find him very open and present in the moment. I feel the trust and the surrender in his vibration. He is not holding on. He has left it all. This is an honor to witness.

I take my hands off. The process is gently ending. He is wrapped up in his element, accepting the healing.

"Take few deep breaths, Jean … a few more. Gently and with no hurry, stretch your body and open your eyes. How are you?" I ask.

"Incredible, Kathy! My hands, Kathy—my hands are very warm."

"Yes. They are red and warm. You accessed the source of healing energy. You did it, Jean."

We sit in silence for a while to allow the healing to take place in total stillness.

"Now look at the sky," I say. "The sun is setting, Jean."

A patch of playful cloud is covering half of the sun—naughty, sweet, bouncy, and beautiful. The cloud does not fear the sun. It is getting closer and closer. The cloud is ready to go through change. Maybe it is time for it to change form and to welcome its new existence. The cloud knows. The cloud is brave and courageous.

I am free. I am ready. I let go. This is the song of the cloud.

I am, I am … I am the change. I am transformation. I am life.

I am neither that patch of traveling white cloud, the icicle hanging from the side of the cliff in fear of melting, nor that drop of rain.

I am neither a lake nor the sea. I am the ocean. I am it all.

I am and I am not at the same time.

I am everything, and I am nothing.

I have the form for a short time, but in my reality, I am formless, shapeless, bodiless, and eternal.

I simply am.

I am in you, and you are in me.

I am love, compassion, passion, kindness, and forgiveness.

I am traveling to reach the light.

I am looking for the sun.

I am open to the change.

I embrace change.

I want change.

* * *

"Hey Jean, let's take a picture of the sunset," I suggest. "Can you take a selfie?"

"I'll try," he says.

We take pictures, but we cannot capture the sunset.

I interpret it this way: we cannot limit the unbounded, unlimited, infinite beauty and joy that we are experiencing now, in this moment, in a picture or two. If and when we want more of this, we must come back to the moment. We must return to this reality in order to see it, feel it, be it, and enjoy it. We cannot fix it and take it with us; we must be present to experience it all in its splendor.

Life is a mandala. Once it is done and completed, the wind of change hits it so very strongly and destroys it. It is vital for us not to get stuck even in the most beautiful of the moments.

Each day is a mini mandala, a sandcastle on the beach. At every sunset, the mandala is completed, awaiting the wave of change to take it back to the source. And the story goes on and on, day after day. Everything—the good, the best, the great, and the unforgettable—meet the angel of change at some point and go back to the origin.

* * *

"Jean, do you remember what you told me while dancing?" I ask. "It completely changed my view about my life in that moment. One of those aha moments in my life!"

"Tell me, what was it, Kathy?"

"While dancing, you caught me looking at the sky and the ocean. You commanded me, in your very own gentle but powerful style, 'Look at me, Kathy. You are dancing with me. You are not dancing with the scenery. I am here.'

"I looked into your eyes, and I found me. I found a woman who did not want to look at any man because she was hurt. She was lost in fear of rejection, betrayal, and deceit. A woman who was not ready to see a man so close to her because she was running away from taking a chance.

"I saw an independent woman, a leader, and for sure not a follower. A woman escaping vulnerability and not ready to be seen. A woman who builds the exit door before building the home.

"In that split second, I found Kathy. I found a woman with so much love and in love with being in love and more in love with being alive. You brought me back to me. In the sanctuary of your safe arms, I faced myself. And I am forever grateful to you.

"I wished for the moment to last forever more, and of course, the hands of the goddess of change were present there too. She gently washed my sandcastle and said to me, 'Kathy, this is your time. This is your moment to dance. Give yourself totally and freely to dance. Don't be afraid. I am here to catch you. I will never lose you.'

"Jean, it was not you talking to me. It was God, the goddess, the angel. I am forever grateful for my first tango lesson. I am ready to dance. I am here to connect, to pause, and to follow!

"You came along to find me and give Kathy back to me. Love you, my friend, forever!"

* * *

I am committed to the Buddha's tango, the dance of awakening.

Today is a gift—an incredible gift of love, trust, and truth. There is a precious sensation in my heart and in my field of energy. Something is shifting. I enjoy the sense of lightness and freedom. I am blessed to be where I am now, and everyone around me can feel my joy and delight.

I loved my first dance lesson with Jean. The gentle but profound movements of the tango mixed with the heat of Kerala and the breeze off the ocean transported me to the realm of fantasy, magic, and miracles once more. Though I had to pay attention to his instructions through the movements, I traveled way beyond body, time, and space.

Kathy follow … trust me and let me take you … I will not lose you, look at me, face me, feel my energy … Wow!

We tell our story in our movements. How you carry your body, the way you walk is how you present yourself to the world. All is shown in your movements. Your story is being told to the universe in your every step. Each move reveals an untold, hidden fact about you. You play the script of your life in each and every gesture without being conscious of it.

You cannot hide who you are from the universe. You are being read at every moment. Every thought, word, and deed is being observed. Your next step follows the previous one.

So be authentic, do not hide, and be available to be explored.

Be passionately in love with life, keep on dancing.

22

The Impermanence

Life is a mystery: solve it.

Today is another exceptional day. It is the last day in Kerala with Jean. He is leaving tomorrow, early morning.

I am having my breakfast in silence. No Ayurveda treatment today. It is a nice day to relax and write. Something in my heart tells me that Jean is not going for his treatment either. He will take the day off too. We can spend the whole day together, since he is leaving tomorrow.

I can see him. He is wearing street clothes and not the green gown as he walks toward the dining hall.

"I did not sleep last night," he says. "I am taking today off."

"I knew it!" I reply.

He smiles. "You know everything about me, don't you?"

"Not everything," I say, "but I know enough." We laugh.

"Okay," he says. "Let us plan our day. Beach, yoga, meditation, shopping, and dance for sure. I want to dance with you to your favorite song. Remember I promised you?" he adds.

When I took the first class with him, he promised me that by the time he leaves, I will know how to tango to "Dance Me to the End of Love."

What is a dance? I think to myself. I define dance as passion taking form and moving in a trance, celebrating the sweet freedom of the soul.

Your inner being shows up, taking uncalculated, spontaneous, improvised steps to meet you at all levels.

I smile, take a deep breath, look into his eyes, and say, "Sure. Sounds good to me."

At the thought of our last dance, an incredible mix of feelings ranging from sadness to joy fills my heart.

* * *

It is time to practice. We walk to the yoga room, ready to play the song and dance to the tune.

"We cannot play music," I realize. "My cell phone does not work here, Jean."

"No worries," he replies. "Let us move to the sound of the waves, take steps to the whisper of the breeze. Connect with me; stay in our cocoon. Follow and do not leave the bubble."

And we begin: one step forward, one step back, and the dance goes on. It is getting easier for me to follow, just because I open up to the idea of being fluid and allowing the steps to take me somewhere where the mind is quiet and does not interfere. Here I can be present, read his energy, and respond. It is easy, effortless, and soft. In response to his energy, I move. No calculation is required. I just need to be present.

People are coming to the yoga room. I get distracted. I cannot follow the steps. I stumble, just like in real life. The moment you feel safe and comfortable, stuff happens.

Who are these people? I cannot focus.

We continue dancing for another few minutes and then leave the room. We are standing on this beautiful open-air platform overlooking the ocean.

"Do you want to dance here, Kathy? Are you comfortable with people watching us?"

"Yes," I tell him. "Here feels better. It is open and beautiful. Yes, let us dance," I say.

I check my phone once more for connection to the internet, and I find the song. Leonard Cohen sings, and I lose myself in his voice. "Dance Me to the End of Love" takes me to the world of sweet connections. We are synchronized, one with each other and one with the song, not knowing where we are going with it.

This is our story: a strong soul-connection, a true friendship, a beautiful dance, a relaxed and uncomplicated flow.

"Wow … incredible," I say when we are done.

"I promised you that you will dance to this song by the time I am leaving," Jean reminded me.

"Yes, Jean, thank you. Yes, you kept your promise!"

We are happy. We are always happy together, and the secret of our connection is not having any expectations. We live one dance at a time. We accept one another exactly the way we are. It feels great to eat, laugh, cry, and dance together for twelve days. Isn't it wonderful?

* * *

"Let's go to the beach," I suggest.

"Sure," he agrees.

We go to the beach for our daily ritual of walking in the water. The waves are crazy and happy to see us together. The ocean knows the truth.

We play in the water. Our clothes get wet. He even loses his cell phone in the ocean, but it seems as if nothing and no one can take away our happiness. This is how harmony looks.

The sun is setting. We watch the sunset in silence and walk back toward the pool. We already miss each other, but we both are quiet about it. Talking about tomorrow will ruin this moment.

Jean wants to go for a swim, and I get into my Zen zone to practice yoga—another part of our daily ritual.

"It is six thirty, Kathy," he says finally. "Time to take a shower and go for dinner. Let's meet at seven thirty."

"Sure," I say. "Come to the restaurant at seven thirty."

* * *

I walk to my room and take a deep breath. I know that tonight will be tough but pleasant. It will be our last dinner together.

I shower, change, and walk very slowly to the restaurant, wearing a beautiful hand-embroidered yellow and black Indian outfit with a gorgeous yellow silk shawl.

"Wow, you look beautiful, Kathy. What a nice color," says Jean.

"Thank you, Jean," I reply. "Tonight is your goodbye dinner. I felt like dressing up."

During dinner, we share an insightful conversation about relationships and take a few pictures to capture the special moments of our exceptional friendship in colors as bright as our connection.

* * *

It is late, and the restaurant is closing. We are the only guests there. Time to say goodnight.

"Well, I guess it is time to say goodbye," says Jean. "I will not see you in the morning because my taxi is taking off at seven thirty. I leave when you are sleeping, Kathy."

"No," I tell him. "I will see you at the restaurant before you go. We will have breakfast together." I speak with a heavy heart. It is difficult not to cry.

"Really, will you be up? What time? I would love to see you in the morning."

"Is six forty-five okay? So as not to eat in a hurry?"

"Six forty-five it is. See you."

I head back to my room … room number 222, where it all began.

I crawl into my bed, thinking wonderful thoughts and feeling utterly grateful for having Jean in my life. I sleep in the arms of my angels. They know how to keep me centered and happy.

Our conversations about how we found each other in India continue dancing in my mind.

Jean wanted to be in Somatheeram in July but there was no opening for him at that time. I needed healing in November after my surgery. He receives a message from the agent that one room is available in November. He already had a plan to visit Japan in November but without hesitation he cancelled travelling to Japan and booked the room in Somatheeram.

Our paths had to cross for some unknown reason and we had to follow the plan of destiny. Our souls had to meet, connect and learn.

Tomorrow is going to be another awesome day, I am sure and off I fly to dreamland!

In this moment all that matters is this precious moment of togetherness, the rest is another sweet mysterious story...

23

For Sure Not the End

Life continues; go with it.

Last night at dinner, a few of the servers were talking with us.

"It is going to be so hard for you guys to part," they said. "You have been here together for almost two weeks all day, every day."

One even told Jean, "When you leave, it will be as if Kathy loses an arm. We are so used to see you both together."

We laughed and joked about their kind comments. It was all so sweet.

* * *

I sleep well. It is five thirty in the morning. I must get up to have time to take a shower. I will meet Jean for breakfast at six forty-five.

I get in the shower not knowing what to expect. What is going to happen today? How will the day unfold? I allow my tears to wash away the heaviness in my heart.

I have a weird feeling in my chest. I am not happy like other days.

It is not easy to define our connection. I feel grateful for the days we had together, knowing soon the time will come to say goodbye. We met totally unplanned and unexpected, and we spent twelve amazing days together, from early morning to late night. We ate, walked on the beach, ran in the water, watched the sunset, drank the nectar of life in every breath, laughed, shared stories, got in and out of yoga poses, and sat in deep meditation. He discovered Reiki, and I explored tango.

Only twelve days. Not a big deal, right?

I must be totally fine. He will be fine. We will be okay.

What am I thinking? Who am I kidding?

I take a deep breath and wipe the tears from my eyes. I am sad, and it is okay.

I pick up my little handbag and key and walk to the dining hall. I get there at six thirty. I am early. The lights are dim.

Breakfast starts at seven. I am by myself, and Jean is not here yet. I choose a table close to the entrance, watching the ocean. These chairs and tables, this room—they all know our story.

I see him coming toward me with a big smile. Our joy, happiness, and childlike giggles fill up the dim and dark space for the last time. The light goes on. We are together again.

"Good morning, Jean!" I say.

"Good morning. How are you doing today?" he asks.

"Great."

His breakfast was ordered the night before, and it is ready. I ask for a cup of special masala Kerala coffee, delicious and comforting.

We eat and talk about future trips together. He promises to watch *The Best Marigold Hotel* movie on the plane.

"See if you can find our characters in that movie," I say.

"Which one do you think is me, Kathy?"

"First you must watch it, and then we will decide on the characters."

More laughter and naughtiness for another few minutes. We are happy to be together.

It is seven thirty. It is time. He must go. The car is waiting for him. We stand in front of each other holding hands.

"You take care of yourself," I say. "Live from your heart, and follow the signs I add."

He says, "I promise, Kathy joon," which in Farsi means *dear Kathy*.

The driver asks if he is from room 222.

"No, I am in 222," I reply. "I am not leaving; he is leaving, and I stay."

In that moment, we look at each other with such joy and say, "Room 222 must be the title of the book and, of course, our movie!"

Room 222 is where the story began. The number *2* is an angel number signifying patience and strength. The angel number *222* means trust, faith, and encouragement. It comes to one's life for a brief pause, suggesting slowing down to reflect. It relates to balance and manifestation of miracles in life.

We pause for a few minutes and look into each other's eyes to register this moment forever, knowing that soon the time will come to say goodbye.

"Goodbye, Jean. I will miss you."

"I will miss you too," he says.

"I love you."

"I love you too."

Three friendly kisses, loving hugs, and a few French words I do not understand end this chapter of our lives. There are goodbyes, smiles, tears, and more goodbyes.

He is in the car now. He rolls the window down. I take a picture of him waving goodbye.

"Hey, Kathy, is this where the story ends?" he asks.

"No. This is the picture of a new beginning," I reply to his comment, showing him the picture of him waving goodbye.

The taxi takes off, packed with our memories. The kind Somatheeram hugs me tenderly, reminding me of the impermanence of our moments. I am sure this old and wise place has witnessed many happy beginnings and many more sad endings. I melt into the arms of my destiny, knowing we are both loved and safe. The ocean is quiet, birds are watching, the rooster is in silence, and we are all in a pause, awaiting the birth of the next chapter.

Jean and I both know "everything must be okay at the end, and if it is not okay, it is not the end," as a character says in the movie.

24

I Love You, India: Almost There but Surely Not Done

Life is a sacred temple; enter it.

It is Christmas Eve, and I am still in Kerala, grateful and extremely happy. The decoration for the evening is stunning at Somatheeram. Colors are breathtaking. The shy dance of the colorful parasols in the wind takes me on the wings of childhood memories.

India is a very special land, and everything is possible here. This is the home of Krishna and Radha, Shiva and Parvati, Ram and Sita. It is the land of gods and goddesses. Here, people worship the sun and honor the moon. This is where the monkey god Hanuman is revered and the mother cow is well respected. This is the birthplace of yoga and the home of Om.

I am here. I am home.

I will be leaving this paradise in two days. Am I ready? I am never ready to leave my beloved India behind. Almost there, but surely not done!

India, I bow in gratitude to all that you have offered me on this magical, life-changing, dreamlike trip of thirty days. During this one month, I met soul mates, rested my mind, purified my soul, and cleansed my body. I connected with you on the deepest level. You were here to listen patiently while I sipped my tea, poured my heart out, and told you my stories. You gently whispered into my ears that you will be here always for me, and I can come back anytime to take shelter in your arms. I can count on your wisdom and deeply rooted teachings forever.

Thank you, India: my home, my love, my teacher, my escape, and my sanctuary. Your mountains have been my refuge in times of pain and sorrow, reminding me of the importance of strength and faith. Your ocean is my source of inspiration and flow. Mother Ganga has been my guru who taught me the power of devotion and dedication for decades.

I learned from you that God is not far from me. I can reach God just by bringing my hands together in a simple Namaste pose, bowing in silence to bless the earth and her children. I learned from you that we are all angels in disguise. We are here to learn, to share, and to serve.

I will be leaving you this time in search of a meaningful love and to find my dance partner for life. Give me your sweet blessings and send me on my journey to magnificence. Bless me to take conscious steps to complete the master bead in the mala of my life.

PS: I love you, Mother India.

25

This Is Me and My Message

Life is and is not: get to know it.

A woman, a mother, a friend, a wife, a sister, a teacher, an engineer, a PhD holder in Esoteric studies, a healer, a yogi, a clinical hypnotherapist, A pianist, a poet, a writer, and a student for life … a refugee, an immigrant, a citizen of the United States … I am all and none of the above.

I am life with all its adventures. I am possibilities awaiting manifestation. I am an active observer of life. Nothing happens to me; I take full responsibility for all of the happenings in my life. I consider myself a blend of karma and free will. I know everything, and I don't know anything at all. More than that, I am and I am not.

Maybe it's because I am a Gemini! Just kidding.

* * *

Allow me to go off track for a moment. I taught yoga and meditation in a prison in Los Angeles for a few years. I had about seventy-five students each time in a class. I was always reminded of being careful in the room around them by different officers in charge. The girls were all in orange-colored uniforms indicating danger.

Being afraid or even worried about anything while in that cold, dark, cement room with one little barred window on the top near its very high ceiling was never an issue for me. I often started the class asking them to introduce themselves one by one. They said their names in a very harsh tone accompanied by tense body language—a sign of protection and fear.

After two or three hours of meditation and spiritual discourse, it was surprising to hear the introduction again. The answer to "Who are you now?" changed every time. Angry Tracy, fearful Mary, revengeful Patty and resentful Caroline had no choice but to leave the room and allow "I am love," "I am a mother," "I am a teacher," and "I am compassion" to take their place. It was a profound shift of energy. The fearful self in the beginning disappeared and loving kindness appeared. This was a profound shift from physical to nonphysical.

Inmates in prison, most of them sentenced to life imprisonment, were allowing a gentle but life-altering move from body to spirit, from form to no form … something to think about! It was quite an honor for me to witness this miracle every time I visited them. In fact, they were my teachers, and I was blessed by them. These girls were not free, but they were unrestricted enough to allow themselves to experience freedom in moments we shared with each other. So *is* and *is not* remains the law governing our lives at every turn.

Where were we? Oh, I was introducing myself!

I was born in Iran in a nonpracticing Muslim family. I lived in Israel for a year and participated in Jewish prayers at the wall of mourning. I was in love with a wonderful Armenian/Gregorian young man while in college. I moved to India and fell in love with Hinduism with all of its mystery and magic of gods and goddesses. I often danced to the tune of Hari Krishna and sat in stillness and awe of the powerful Om Nama Shivaya chant.

I immersed myself in the teachings of Vedas, Upanishad, and Patanjali yoga sutras. I married a Sikh at the age of twenty-four and spent most Sundays at the local Gurudwara listening to Kirtan and studied Guru Granth Sahib. I traveled to Tibet, fell at the feet of Buddha, and was embraced by the mercy of Quan Yin. I am a dedicated student of Lao Tzu, studying the life-transforming Tao Te Ching for decades.

As you can clearly see, I am pretty open and welcoming to all religions. By the way, I forgot to tell you that I was married for eleven years to an Irish/Italian Catholic man from New York City.

From a very young age, I was totally fascinated with and exposed to all religions and beliefs. I never felt one was right and the other was wrong. I studied the core of each one and did not judge the teachings by people's behavior. I believe my numerous past-life experiences came in handy this time around. Feeling comfortable in the mosque, temple, Gurudwara, church, or synagogue was a gift growing up.

Another interesting part of my life has been living in many different countries and cities. Let me count. Ready? I was born and lived in Iran; lived in Israel for a year because of my dad's job; moved to India at the age of twenty-three; and lived in London and Frankfurt after I got married to Banka. Then we moved together to Chicago and from there to San Diego, San Jose, Los Angeles, and few years later found ourselves living in Dubai. After five years in Dubai, we decided to return to the United States and settle down in Houston, Texas. That did not last long; after six months, we moved back to California. After I got married for the second time, I moved to Connecticut, and four years later moved back to California.

What a spin! Don't you feel dizzy just by reading it?

I have been living in heavenly Orange County, California, since 2011, and I love it. I have traveled and visited many parts of the world for various spiritual reasons, from Brazil to China, India, Tibet, Thailand, Malaysia, most of Europe, Dubai, Canada, Costa Rica, Mexico, Singapore, Greece, and many more. As my dad used to say, "You have wheels under your feet." Yes, I think I have! I am a traveler, a wanderer. Currently the name of my street is "Gitano" which means Gypsy! How about that? Nothing is a coincidence.

A spiritual life is definitely not a black-and-white exposé; it is a colorful experience. It does not bind you to either this or that. It is this and that combined, melting into each other and emerging as one. As a meditation lover, I find it is so comforting to sit in stillness for hours, but there are other ways to meditate as well. Be open to dance and express your feelings, embodying movements. Arrange a flowerpot and tell your story with colors. Experience life in all forms of offerings. Do not limit yourself to reading one type of book or practicing one style of yoga or simply meditating and chanting. Open yourself up to the magic of singing and dancing, painting and cooking, and all other kinds of activities that allow you to express your inner essence and show who you really are.

Do not limit yourself by labeling your path as a Buddhist, Christian, or Hindu. Choose to be a Buddha, be the light of Christ, and live as Krishna. Buddha was never a Buddhist; he was simply awake, and so you can be. Life is grand and limitless. Live on the edge, be excited to be alive, and renew the self, one breath at a time passionately.

Labels and titles give form to life. Always remember: life is shapeless and formless, with no beginning and no end. It is a sacred experience of vibrations and emotions to be all and to do more. Do not waste this precious but very short endeavor. Get out there and create memories to last a lifetime and beyond—just because you can.

Know that you are the person you are looking for. Look in to your eyes in the mirror and search for the truth within. Once you find yourself you find solace and contentment. Keep looking for the self, the most important being in your life.

I have been asked many times: what did you learn traveling and living among different cultures? Wasn't it difficult to adjust? Traveling all around the world and living in many parts of it with different cultures is the most exciting and enlightening part of my life. I learned a simple truth: the sky is the same color, and the core of people is one everywhere. I believe that we are one spirit living in countless bodies: the mother tongue, the food, the religion, or the traditions might differ, but the language of the heart is known to all. Wherever you go, there you are!

I found pieces of me in different cultures and traditions. I learned that I do not end when he or she begins. I learned oneness and togetherness and allowed myself to melt the restrictions and limitations. I learned not to look for the extraordinary, in fact I found the ordinary me who cries when someone is in pain and laughs at simple jokes.

Find that ordinary man or woman who is shy at times and bold in other occasions. Be in search of the one who stumbles while dancing in the rain and sings awful in the shower. Laugh and be silly. Find happiness in your simple abundance. Most importantly know that you are enough. There is no becoming. You are who you have been always looking for.

I found it impossible to escape the self, and the thirst for spiritual growth followed me everywhere. I also learned to find my element and my place in the world and make the space mine. Accepting different cultures and being comfortable with them is a blessing I must not ignore.

Living in peace among different colors and creeds is a privilege and not a curse. You must be super-lucky to share this amazing life with people of different cultures, customs, religions, and social norms. To accept more and to be more is the gift of being exposed to people sharing this planet with us.

Religions and spiritual masters, to me, are different chapters of the same book. They share a common message. None of them is the end of teachings. The more you learn, the less you know. They expand our mind to explore the realm beyond the limited world of matter. They all believe in one common fact: we are part of LOVE.

Yes, we are pieces of that intelligence, that unlimited and infinite source of being in a form for just a short while. We are carrying messages—significant messages that we must deliver. I encourage you to surrender to the reality beyond the restricted world of form and matter. The vibration of the act of surrender can take you on a magic carpet ride to visit the angels, ascended masters, divine beings of light, and ultimately, the source of all that is. Mind you, my friend: once you touch that reality, your story begins.

All spiritual teachings build the first step to self-searching. To know you and to be you is the ultimate goal of this life on earth. Being religious or nonreligious is just a game—a label that does not matter. Go beyond rules and laws; be free to search, to find, and to share. This is your homework while in body. Your message is unique, interesting, and needs to be heard. Explore it, understand it, and share it.

You are as important as the Buddha. Your life is as significant as the life of Christ. You are as loved as Krishna and Ram. As long as you live your truth, your name does not matter to the source of consciousness. To the fountain of love and compassion, you are as important as Zoroaster and Moses.

Do not box yourself; do not limit yourself. Remember: you have a set of unclipped wings, ready to fly, and this is your chance to soar. Get off that sofa. Get out of that dead relationship. Quit that useless job. Dare more and be more. Open that door and live your life in the fullest volume. Do not settle for less.

You are what this world needs. Offer your wisdom, peace, and compassion to this chaotic world. Mother Earth is in need of tender loving care, and no one can give it to her better than you. Do not wait for a famous person or a leader to do the job. Get out of your way and do it. Show up and be you. Play the part, and confirm that you are not separated from the unlimited, infinite, and unrestricted source of possibilities. Make a commitment to serve the light in your own specific and unique way.

Do not wait to become; you already are, and you are enough. All you can do is be *you* and allow *me* to be *me*. Be courteous, patient, and loving toward all life on earth. Respect the earth, water, plants, animals, and people. We are sharing this beautiful planet, and we all matter. No one is more important than the other one. The crow, the eagle, the ocean, the ant, the bees and the birds, the tall oak tree, and the tiny blade of grass are dancing to the tune of life. They are deeply in love with their own lives. Honor them and be honored by them. Consciously choose peace as your occupation, your trade, and your mantra.

You and I are in charge of peace on earth. No one can give it to us; we must create it. No one is going to give women freedom. We are born free. Who are they to give us freedom? We are free beings of light. So be it. People of color, you are beautiful, and you make this planet a remarkable place to live. You bring the significance of colors into the world. Accept yourself and love who you really are.

Our spirit has no color. It is neither black nor white. It is luminous and transparent, so don't waste time fighting the ones who cannot see your grandeur.

We continue the journey of life believing in our power and strength. Never do something from the point of fear. It will end in disaster. Discover your center by simply being honest to yourself. Find yourself, meet the self, and get to know the infinite self who is residing in this finite body.

Learn more about your essence that has no gender, no color, and no shape. Understand your message, believe in it, share it, own it, and live it. Be the Buddha, be Mahatma, be the guru, live as a master. Buddha was not a Buddhist; he was the server of light, and so you can be.

Stay far away from the ones calling themselves masters. They know nothing. Their ego is loud and deafening. Remember the Tao's teaching: "Once the wise man said nothing."

If you are facing an obstacle in your life, consider yourself the luckiest among all. See the obstacle as your path to rise above it. Practice forgiveness while going through divorce; find tenderness facing death of a loved one;

introduce peace to war and devastation; stay kind in the face of anger; foster strength when confronted by fear. Simply turn on the light in the chamber of darkness.

Be kind to unkind people. Be fair to unfair ones, teaching them the other side of living. Be honest in your words, loving in your thoughts, and present in your actions. Never blame others. Always be accountable for what is going on in your life—only then will you find courage to let go and move on. Lose the victim's hat; it does not suit you. Instead, choose to wear the crown of a master. Remember Jean and the importance of following. Follow the inner guidance, and you will be there.

In your actions lives your message. Show up in your life and write the lyrics of the most unique song to tango. Call it "My Life, My Message"

Make the dance yours. Be creative and take unstructured steps. Surprise yourself by always being new and unpredictable. Be bold, live on the edge, and enjoy the thrill of life by being unpredictable. Dress in your experiences. Add a flavor of ancient teachings into your modern day-to-day life. Wear it. Let your hair down.

Do not wait for an invitation to dance; instead, get up and follow your heart to the stage, hold life in your arms, and lose yourself in the arms of life passionately. Do not be consumed by what other people—teachers or self-called masters—say or said. Be your own master.

You are Natraj in form, the Lord of Dance. Hold the fire of knowledge and move passionately to the inner song of yours. Listen! The music is playing. Stand on a lotus flower surrounded by the flame of awareness, lifting one leg off to balance on the demon of ignorance.

Cheers, Om, and Namaste to the world!

And *The Buddha's Tango* in you continues. One step forward, one step back. Embrace, Connect, pause, Feel, and follow. Breath by breath, day by day, life after life, keep on dancing, *Tango On!* Just because you can.

This is not the end for sure. Till we meet again!

26

Now It Is Your Turn to Write

My message is...

Write about your life's message and the steps you must take to deliver it. If you are not clear about it, simply hold a pen in your hands and place it on your heart chakra. Close your eyes, center yourself by connecting to Mother Earth, and allow the words to stream out from your subconscious mind into the pen and onto the blank page.

Don't question the message; just write the words. When you read it later, it will make total sense. Go beyond everyday life to get to the core of your existence. This is where your message is engraved. Trust your intuition and bring it to the surface.

Each word carries your feelings and emotions. Ground yourself and stay in the moment to feel the vibration of each word to the fullest. This is your authentic self who is writing. Trust the flow! Write it, date it, and follow the signs to bring it to life.

Live your message, because you matter.

My message

My message

My message

My message

My message

My Mom and Dad…the glamorous couple

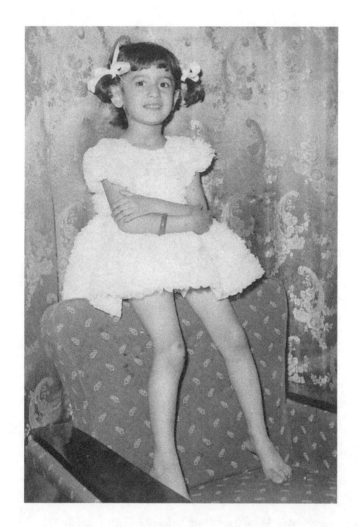

Me age 4…getting ready to face life!

My brother Ali Reza, myself at age 9, my sister Kianoush. This is when it all began!

With my dear grandfather (Agha joon) age 4

I am in Heaven... age 14 ...Tango with Dad!

Of course my Frosty boy and me!

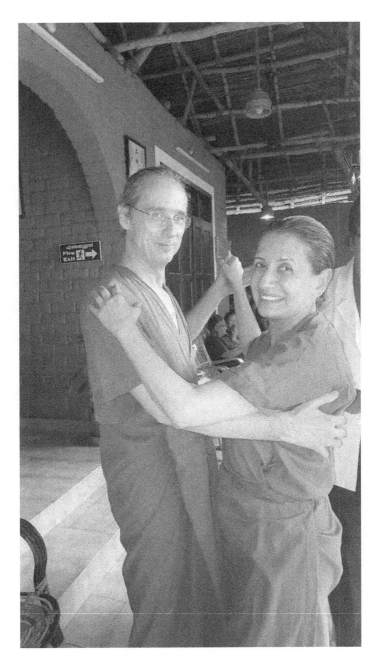

*With Jean in India at the Ayurveda center.
In our funny treatment gowns!*

Last but not least… Me and Omid (my son) in
Tango…This is called True Happiness!

CPSIA information can be obtained
at www.ICGtesting.com
Printed in the USA
BVHW041038080719
552848BV00010B/324/P